PERMANENT
Parisians

AN ILLUSTRATED, BIOGRAPHICAL
GUIDE TO THE CEMETERIES
OF PARIS

JUDI CULBERTSON
& TOM RANDALL

ROBSON BOOKS

First published in Great Britain in 1991 by Robson Books,
10 Blenheim Court, Brewery Road, London N7 9NT

A member of the Chrysalis Group plc

This edition first published by Robson Books in 2000

British Library Cataloguing in Publication Data
A catalogue record for this title is available from the British Library

ISBN 1 86105 336 3

Printed by Redwood Books, Trowbridge ,Wiltshire

This book is dedicated to our parents

Charlotte and Hubert
Muriel and Harold

and to our son, Andrew,

with love.

CONTENTS

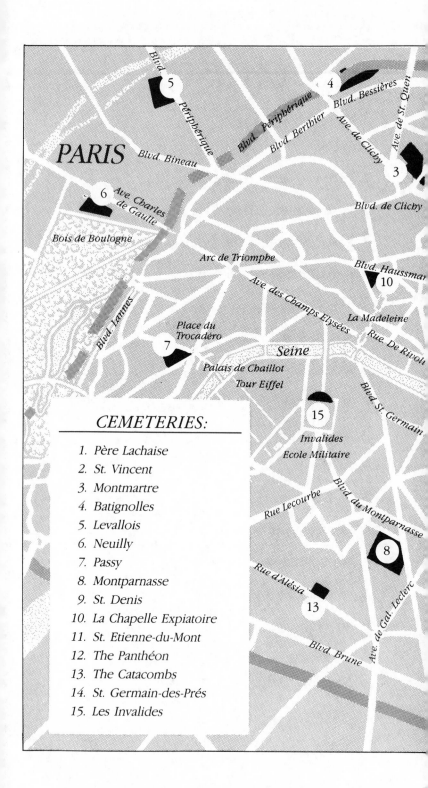

PARIS

Blvd. Périphérique
Blvd. Bineau
Blvd. Berthier
Blvd. Bessières
Ave. de St. Quen
Ave. de Clichy
Blvd. de Clichy
Ave. Charles de Gaulle
Bois de Boulogne
Arc de Triomphe
Blvd. Haussman
Ave. des Champs Elysées
La Madeleine
Blvd. Lannes
Place du Trocadéro
Rue De Rivoli
Seine
Palais de Chaillot
Tour Eiffel
Blvd. St. Germain
Invalides
Ecole Militaire
Rue Lecourbe
Blvd. du Montparnasse
Rue d'Alésia
Rue de Gal. Leclerc
Blvd. Brune

CEMETERIES:

1. Père Lachaise
2. St. Vincent
3. Montmartre
4. Batignolles
5. Levallois
6. Neuilly
7. Passy
8. Montparnasse
9. St. Denis
10. La Chapelle Expiatoire
11. St. Etienne-du-Mont
12. The Panthéon
13. The Catacombs
14. St. Germain-des-Prés
15. Les Invalides

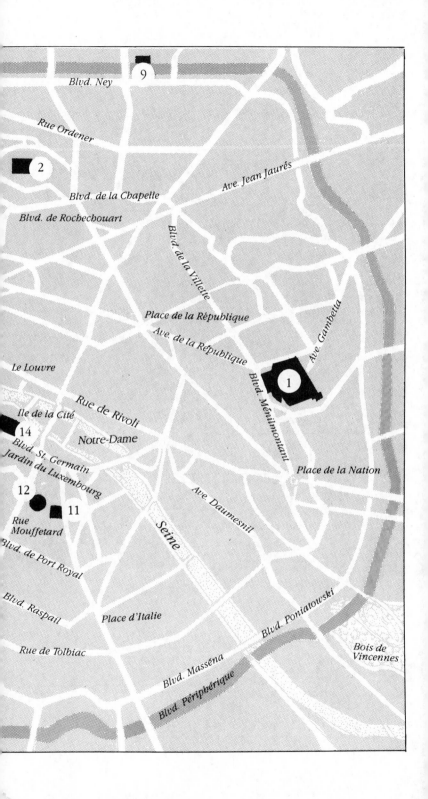

PREFACE

▲ ▲ ▲

I seldom go out, but when I feel myself flagging I go and cheer myself up in Père Lachaise . . . while seeking out the dead I see nothing but the living.

—BALZAC

PARIS IS FAMOUS for her croissants, her art treasures, and her general cachet, but perhaps she is less well known for her necrography. Yet nothing illustrates the slender line between life and death so well as the cemeteries of Paris. Stone figures seem to start up from their beds as if hearing a noise, or dance as if they had been turned to marble without warning. To visit these burial grounds is to be struck with wonder.

There is little depressing about French cemeteries. Although the three or four hundred cats of Père Lachaise lie low during the day, its passages are alive with gatekeepers, picnickers, and tourists looking for famous names. Such names are around every corner. Here is Chopin, there Gertrude Stein. Among those buried in Père Lachaise alone are Marcel Proust, Oscar Wilde, Sarah Bernhardt, Isadora Duncan, Auguste Comte, Georges Seurat, Edith Piaf, and Héloïse and Abélard.

Across town in Montmartre lie impressionist Edgar Degas and writers Alexandre Dumas (fils), Heinrich Heine, and Emile Zola. Farther south in Montparnasse are such recent arrivals as Jean Seberg and Jean-Paul Sartre and old-timers like Maupassant, Saint-Saëns, and Alfred Dreyfus. National treasures and military heros such as Voltaire, Rousseau, Victor Hugo, and, of course, Napoléon are

Opposite: Père Lachaise pathway

1

Permanent Parisians

buried in the Panthéon and Les Invalides.

From the tombs of the early kings Childeric and Dagobert to the mass graves of French Revolution victims, the history of France has been carved in stone. And while one object of a book like this is certainly to offer historical background, its main purpose is to focus on the lives of notable people who, by accident or design, have remained in Paris permanently. These people range from the very

famous down to certain anonymous souls whose memorial statuary has made them more famous dead than alive.

In choosing who would merit a full-length portrait rather than just an honorable mention, we selected, along with the Voltaires and Victor Hugos, others who were cultural forces in their times. We also chose those whose lives and deaths were particularly interesting, as well as people who are better known to Americans than some of their contemporaries. There were several we wanted to include but could not locate: Richard Wright, who is supposedly buried somewhere in Père Lachaise, and Rabelais who, along with Mozart's mother, was interred in a churchyard which has vanished.

A statistically minded reader might notice that there are more painters than generals. And he would be right. Though we tried to be fair, in the end we chose the people we wanted. The generals, minor scientists, and politicians have been covered by shorter descriptive paragraphs; indeed, because of the astonishing wealth of these burial grounds, most of the people and monuments in the book have been treated that way.

In Europe an interest in cemeteries is not regarded as morbid or unnatural. On November first and second, thousands of Parisians flock to Père Lachaise to celebrate All Saints Day and the Day of the Dead. Much French funerary sculpture is designed to be appreciated (and sometimes to give a warning or impart a private joke). The French also find inspiration in pausing at the grave of someone long-admired and leaving flowers there.

We have arranged the book by cemeteries, opening each chapter with a general description followed by a cemetery tour of the monuments and inhabitants, providing short biographies for those of greatest significance. The arrangement of the chapters is roughly geographical, though Paris herself resists such petty attempts at order. For the larger cemeteries original maps are included which suggest a walking tour and show the important graves specifically located in each division—a must in such places as Père Lachaise, where most divisions contain hundreds of monuments! But although the size of the larger cemeteries may seem initially daunting, it also increases your chance of stumbling on something beautiful or poignant or shocking which we may have missed.

In any case, bonne exploration!

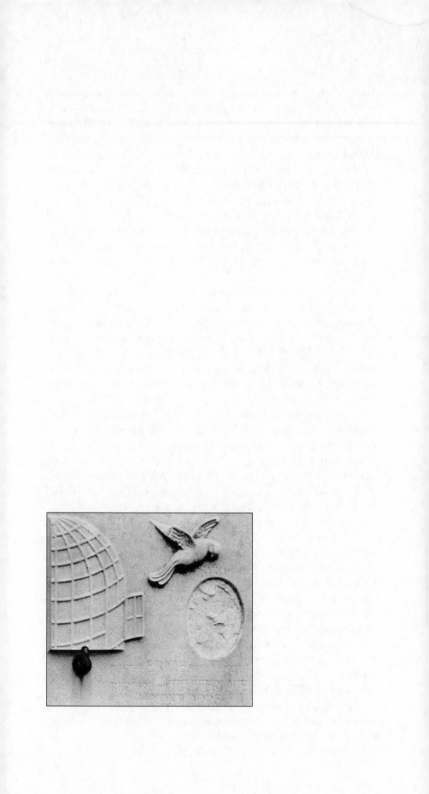

PÈRE LACHAISE *Overview*

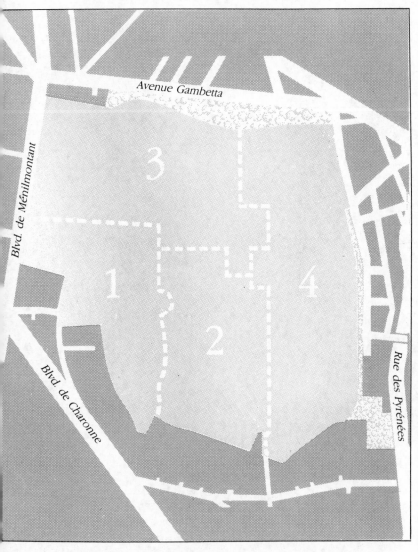

C H A P T E R   1

PÈRE LACHAISE
Tour One

▲   ▲   ▲

*To be buried in Père Lachaise is
like having mahogany furniture.*
—VICTOR HUGO

THE LARGER CEMETERIES of Paris, though built like small cities, resemble European campgrounds even more. There is the same crowded feeling of people who have pitched their tents in every available space and are untroubled by the closeness of others, the sense that any private rituals will be tactfully ignored by one's neighbors. Although Père Lachaise is considered a garden cemetery, its interior roads are curiously metropolitan, lined with stone shelters and marked with street signs.

The oldest of the existing cemeteries, Père Lachaise, opened in 1804 at the behest of Napoléon (who became Emperor the same week). At that point Paris was in desperate need of new burial places. Skeletons protruding from churchyard ground could be seen by passersby, and pressure from the two thousand bodies in Cimetière des Innocents had broken through an adjacent apartment house wall, spewing corpses into its basement. After the scandal broke—and the odor nearly asphixiated local residents—legislation closed city cemeteries and churchyards to further burials. A quarry south of Paris was opened in 1786 to store the overflow of bones.

But although anonymous burial may have been suitable for transferred bones, it was not a very appealing way to bid au revoir to one's loved ones, and proposals for alternatives were soon underway. Working quickly, urban planner Ni-

Opposite: Frédéric Chopin

- Ⓐ Colette
- Ⓑ Gioacchino Rossini
- Ⓒ Alfred de Musset
- Ⓓ Baron Haussmann
- Ⓔ François Arago
- Ⓕ Jules Romains
  Mlle. Lenormand
- Ⓖ Rachel
- Ⓗ Rothschild Family
- Ⓘ Camille Pissarro
- Ⓙ Héloïse and Abélard
- Ⓚ Francis Poulenc
- Ⓝ Georges Rodenbach
- Ⓟ Ferdinand de Lesseps
- Ⓠ Jim Morrison
- Ⓡ Rémy de Gourmont
- Ⓢ Frédéric Chopin
- Ⓣ Luigi Cherubini
- Ⓤ Vincenzo Bellini
- Ⓥ Gabriel Pierné
- Ⓦ Sophie Blanchard
- Ⓧ Ginette Neveu
- Ⓨ Théodore Géricault
- Ⓩ François Joseph Talma
- ⓐ Edouard Branly
- ⓑ Mlle George

cholas Frochot purchased land that had originally belonged to Louis XIV's confessor, Père Lachaise, and was then owned by a Baron Desfontaines. (Frochot was persuasive in ways that may not have been recorded: not only did he talk Desfontaines into selling for a very low price and vacating the land in eight days, he resold him a piece of cemetery property 18 years later at 282 times the original sale price!)

In the beginning, bodies did not flock to the new Cimetière de l'Est. To give his cemetery more cachet, Frochot arranged the reburial there of celebrated authors Molière and La Fontaine. A few years later he also recruited Héloïse and Abélard. Other cemeteries had begun opening, but by then Père Lachaise was firmly established as the most prestigious; up to the present it has remained the preferred resting place for those who can afford its high tariffs. Frochot himself is buried in Division 37.

The principal entrance to Père Lachaise is on the Boulevard de Menilmontant, but a more successful way to explore its 118 acres is to take the Métro to Gambretta stop, walk down Avenue du Père Lachaise and enter at Rue des Rondeaux. Although this puts you at the back of the cemetery, it also puts you at the top and allows you to walk more or less downhill, catching the Métro at stop Père Lachaise.

How you choose to explore this cemetery is an individual matter. Considering its vast number of famous people and the particular interests of each visitor, it would be

PÈRE LACHAISE: Tour One

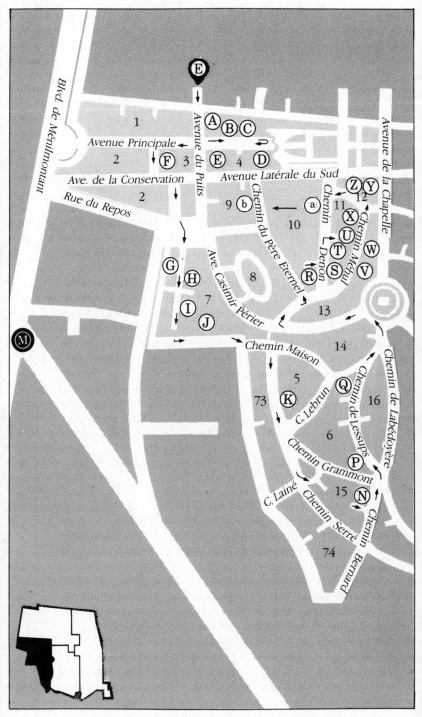

useless to set up a fixed itinerary. Rather, we have listed in numerical order the divisions that have interesting people or graves and have suggested some possible routes to follow on the map.

DIVISION 1

In this section are the monuments of **Gustave Froment** (1815–1865), the scientist who created the gyroscope and the electric dial telegraph; and **Louis Lemaire** (1824–1910), a painter whose tomb resembles the pyramid on the back of a one-dollar bill.

DIVISION 3

Here lies **Jules Romains** (1885–1972), the author of *Men of Good Will*, a monumental work of fiction (27 volumes) whose settings range across Europe between 1908 and 1933.

Ernest Archdeacon (1862–1950), an Irish lawyer who turned his back on Old Bailey to pursue a passion for aviation and the automobile. He set several ballooning records (including one in 1885 for going 75 mph during a gale) and was part of Lindbergh's welcoming committee. In later years he advocated a universal language, Esperanto, also the name of his houseboat on the Seine.

Marie Lenormand (1772–1843), a fortuneteller whose working name was La Sibylle du Faubourg Saint-Germain. She was consulted by Joséphine just before she met Napoléon, and is supposed to have told the future Empress that if she played her cards right she would be "more than a queen."

DIVISION 4

This division (see map) is easy to explore, since most of its important people are facing each other along the Avenue Principale. Starting on the right and working around the loop, you will find:

François Arago (1786–1853), a scientist who determined planetary diameters and pioneered in electromagnatism and theories on light. In his spare time he worked to abolish slavery in the French colonies. Arago's well-elevated bronze bust depicts the features of a reformer.

Thomas Couture (1815–1879), an academic painter who dismissed his contemporaries as "daubers" and "drunken clowns" and threw Manet out of his studio for persisting in trying to paint the models wearing clothes instead of classically nude. Couture's bust, flanked by two admiring cher-

View of Thomas Couture's bust

ubs, is located at the foot of Félix Faure.

Félix Faure (1841–1899), the sixth president of the French Republic who, in true Belle Epoque spirit, died in the arms of his mistress—endearing him to the French populace in a way that his policies never did. His bronze figure is raised slightly and turning as if, waking, he can't figure out where his paramour has gone.

Alfred de Musset and Mme Lardin de Musset

Baron Georges Eugène Haussmann (1809–1891), a prefect who reconstructed and modernized Paris, widening roads and abolishing huge picturesque sections of the city in the process. His plan was to abolish the Parisian cemeteries as well and relocate everyone on a five thousand acre site 14 miles outside Paris (with special "funeral trains" to carry the coffins and mourners). Parisians successfully resisted that idea. His own mausoleum has a rusted door and looks sadly uncared for.

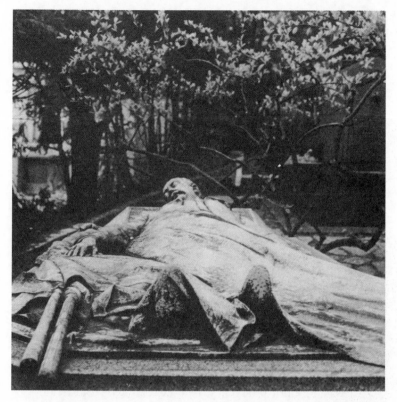

Félix Faure

Alfred de Musset (1810–1857), a poet whose finest verses were composed after an unhappy love affair with George Sand (Amadine Aurora Lucie). His sheltered bust looks out over Avenue Principale and partially hides the tomb of his sister, **Mme Lardin de Musset** (1819–1905), who is located behind him. Also a poet, she is depicted sitting in a chair and holding a book on her lap.

The empty tomb of composer **Gioacchino Rossini** (1792–1868). No, he is not risen, simply moved to Florence in 1887. He leaves behind a plain stone monument.

Paul Albert Bartholmé (1848–1928), a painter until his beloved wife died of cancer and his friend Edgar Degas encouraged him to create a sculpture for her grave. It was so successful that he continued in this medium, culminating his triumphs with the huge *Monument aux Morts* (Monument to the Dead) which dominates the end of Avenue Principale in this section. His tomb is located opposite that of Félix Faure.

Finally, loved by many Americans, the author:

SIDONIE GABRIELLE COLETTE *b. January 28, 1873, Saint-Sauveur; d. August 3, 1954, Paris.* When Colette died in 1954 and was refused a Catholic burial, there was an immediate uproar. How dare the Church deny her such consolation, just because she had been married three times? Whatever had happened to Christian charity? Actually, it is doubtful whether Colette herself would have cared. The author of *Gigi* and *Claudine at School* was never concerned with conventional morality. Indeed, her plain granite tomb fits like a mattress into a large black frame and resembles nothing so much as a double bed—a shrewd metaphor for sensual pleasures.

Colette's mother, "Sidu," adored her youngest child and was devastated when she left their country home in 1893 to marry an older man, Henri Gauthier-Villars. Part of the Colette legend is that "Willy" locked her in her room and made her write; what is less well known is that he touched up her stories and published them under his own name. Although the books' heroine, Claudine, was Colette's creation, she obediently added the schoolgirl-teacher romances which Willy suggested would make the books sell better.

It was not until 1904 that Colette was allowed to use her own name to publish *Dialogues des Bêtes*, an entertainment about animals. By then she and Willy were increasingly at odds, and she was tired of his extramarital affairs. To support herself Colette trained as a mime and toured the country, happily baring her breasts when the script demanded it. At this time she also began to write seriously.

When Colette was nearly 40, she found to her surprise that she was pregnant. She married her lover, Henri de Jouvenel (another writer), and their daughter, also Colette, was born in July, 1913. Colette loved "Bel Gazou" increasingly as she turned from "a run-of-the-mill baby into a little girl and from a little girl into my daughter," but they never developed the kind of closeness she had had with her own mother to whom she wrote every day.

The marriage ended in 1924 when she divorced de Jouvenel for infidelity. As always, her life was reflected in her writing. Its themes change over the years from older man-young girl romances to those of young men with experienced women, as in *Chéri*. In 1935 Colette married a man 15 years her junior, Maurice Goudeket. This time the marriage took.

Colette's attitudes toward life and conventional morality

were curiously unschooled, free from preconceptions of "normal behavior." Her writing emerges unfiltered and evocative, involving the physical senses as well as the heart.

Shortly before she died, she wrote, "Depending on whether my bed, which follows me like the shell of a snail, is placed at one or the other window, I may or may not chance to spy certain stars familiar to a nephew of mine . . . . When the stars he has pointed out to me are not apparent from my vantage point, I invent them and stick them up where they are not. For one who can barely stir, it's easy to confuse the stern order of the universe by craning one's neck.

" 'We don't have any Great Bear here,' remarked one of my neighbors.

"She added in the same pinched tone: 'We're very badly off for fish shops in the first arrondissement.' "

Even when invoking the grandeur of nature, Colette never forgot the human touch.

DIVISION 5

Directly on Chemin Serre near its intersection with Chemin Lebrun stands the small, neat mausoleum and bright stained-glass window of **Francis Poulenc** (1889–1963). Originally the "clown" and once the most underrated of the composers known as Les Six (Arthur Honegger, Darius Milhaud, George Auric, Louis Duray, and Germaine Tailleferre), Poulenc is now considered the strongest and most original of that group. In his youth his music poked fun at older composers. A great writer of songs, he also wrote well-crafted, appealing orchestral pieces such as *Aubade* and the ballet score *Les Biches* (The Deer).

In later years his works grew more serious and even religious, culminating in his *Gloria* (1961) and his opera *Les Dialogues des Carmélites* (1957) which has enjoyed recent revival and popularity. To some who knew him, his manner did not match his Fernandel-like smile and the wit of his music, but it is his unique and moving music that we have been left to enjoy.

DIVISION 6

The pyramid-shaped tomb of **Ferdinand de Lesseps** (1805–1894) reflects his finest achievement, the Suez Canal. Although he was ultimately successful in completing it, his rival the Duc de Morny, who was acting secretly for British interests, tried to take over the concession. De Morny attempted first to have de Lesseps discredited as incompetent, then tried to frighten stockholders into dumping their shares so he could buy them up cheaply. Justice prevailed, de Morny was exposed, and the canal opened successfully in 1869.

Now faced with rivalry of a different sort, de Lesseps shares the division with one of the most adored tombs in the cemetery: Jim Morrison's. The graffiti from this tomb spills over onto those of its neighbors', forming a small neighborhood where Morrison's worshippers, teenagers from numerous countries, gather. His bust is often surrounded with empty wine and beer bottles into which flowers have been placed. The face has recently been painted white with red lips and black hair. The graffiti ranges from names and slogans to Morrison's lyrics, and quotes from other writings his followers find meaningful. Long before you come to the tomb you find white arrows with "Jim" painted on the sides of monuments pointing the way, and as you near it, the gathering of adolescents assures that you will not miss the location.

JAMES DOUGLAS MORRISON b. *December 8, 1943, Melbourne, Florida; d. July 3, 1971, Paris.* Despite his flirtations with death, it is doubtful that Jim Morrison, penning his famous lyric "No one here gets out alive," ever expected to be entombed so early—and in a country where he didn't even speak the language. If, indeed, that is what happened. Fourteen years later his death is still an enigma.

Jim was born into a patriotic American family, the first child of a young naval career couple. From the beginning he had an IQ of 149 and a tendency toward anarchy, which was perhaps compounded by the instability of his family's constant moves around the country. As an adolescent, while his father advanced to command the three thousand men of the *Bon Homme Richard,* Jim was trying out different personas—serious poet, heavy drinker, brilliant philosophy student, and public nuisance.

At UCLA Morrison became involved in music as an afterthought, but he soon gained fame as the lead singer and songwriter for a rock group, The Doors. Portraying himself as a "backdoor man," he kindled a flame in the youth of America—though not in his own family.

Jim Morrison's popularity soared between 1967 and 1970, but he spent his last months in Paris trying to find himself and pull his life into shape. He loved the city with its echoes of his heroes Sartre and Baudelaire and the respite he found there from public recognition. Yet he often felt compelled to draw attention to himself when he wasn't recognized, and his chronic alcoholism persisted.

On Monday morning, July 5, 1971, the rumor started that

Jim Morrison was dead. Bill Siddon, manager of The Doors, called Jim's wife Pamela from Los Angeles to confirm it, then left for Paris. When he arrived she showed him a sealed coffin and a signed death certificate; allegedly Jim had died in the bathtub of a heart attack. The next day the coffin was secretly buried in Père Lachaise, leaving behind millions of grieving fans and almost as many questions. Pamela Morrison, the only witness, died three years later in a car crash in Africa.

A decade later, little has changed. Adolescents who were toddlers in 1971 now hold vigils at his grave. But whether Jim Morrison is actually buried there no one can say. No autopsy was done; Pamela "could not remember" the name of the doctor who had signed the certificate. And Jim had fantasized about telling the world he was dead and starting a new life elsewhere. He had planned to contact his office by an anagram-name he had devised: Mr. Mojo Risin'.

His fans are still waiting. But so far Mr. Mojo has not come forward.

DIVISION 7

This section was originally reserved for Jewish burials. The pleasant but plain mausoleum on the right is that of the actress **Rachel** (Elisa Félix, 1820–1858), one of the greatest tragediennes of the century. She first attracted an audience by singing for bread on the streets of Lyons. Though she later drew inspiration from her unhappy childhood, she never quite overcame its effects. Her greatest success came in the plays of Racine and Corneille, particularly *Phaedre*. An exhausting tour of the United States, combined with her feverish pursuit of love affairs hastened Rachel's death from tuberculosis at 38.

Across the street to the right is the French branch of the banking **Rothschilds**. The monument is a large, deep mausoleum with names inscribed on the wall of a corridor leading to its interior; the family's name does not appear on the mausoleum's outside.

Up a slight incline is the mournful facade of **Jacob Robles**, an otherwise unknown personality, whose face and gesture of finger to his lips impose a doleful silence on passersby. Near to him is the grave of impressionist painter:

CAMILLE PISSARRO *b. July 10, 1830, St. Thomas, West Indies; d. November 13, 1903, Paris.* In impressionist exhibits some styles are easily recognized: the softness of Monet, the studied pointillism of Seurat, the angularity of Cézanne, the turbulent brilliance of Van Gogh. Other artists, such as Degas and Gauguin, are also identifiable by their subject matter. But there is a third category: those artists whose paintings were admired during their lifetimes, but who left no trademarks for posterity.

One of these was Camille Pissarro. Certainly no one worked harder year after year organizing the exhibits of "Independents," or was kinder or more encouraging to younger artists. With his white beard, wire glasses, and black hat, he fell easily into the patriarchal role. Yet he could never quite shake off the influence of others and break away to a style all his own.

Pissarro had another handicap, a buxom shrew for a wife. Formerly a maid in his parents' home, Julie kept waiting for him to abandon painting and get "a real job." She nagged him ceaselessly about money and was furious when five of their seven children became artists.

She did have a point, of course: in the beginning no one willingly bought impressionist art. Renoir once stopped by the home of a patron with a new work, only to be told that he was too late, that Pissarro had already been there and sold a painting "because he has such a large family, poor chap." Renoir, incensed, demanded later of a friend, "Just because I'm a bachelor and have no children, am I to die of starvation? I'm in just as tight a corner as Pissarro, yet when they talk of me, no one says, 'That poor Renoir.'"

When Pissarro was 60, he finally began to sell his paintings at better prices. He wanted to return to London where he had gained much of his inspiration in the past, but Julie refused to move. She pressured him to buy the house they had rented for years at Eragny (about 45 miles northwest of Paris) and he finally did so, borrowing money from Monet. At this point he was also supporting his painter sons and their wives.

Pissarro had trouble with eye infections for many years, but his health was otherwise good, and when he developed an abscess of the prostate gland at 73 his doctor attempted to treat it homeopathically. The infection spread through

his system, and the artist died of blood poisoning. He left behind a large, loving family and two successful prodigies, Cézanne and Gauguin—not bad by-products for one whose lifetime motto was "Only painting counts."

Finally, up on a hill in an uncrowded area all their own, are two of the cemetery's best-known residents: Abélard and Héloïse. The monument is a raised tomb depicting the couple supine in prayer. A plaque on the base outlines their history, and covering them is a structure which resembles

an ornate gazebo. The entire monument is fenced in, perhaps to discourage the lovelorn from taking souvenirs.

PETER ABÉLARD *(1079 – 1142)* and **HÉLOÏSE** *(ca. 1101– 1164)*.

> As Abélard said to Héloïse, 'Don't forget to drop a line to me, please.'

Cole Porter's irreverent introduction to "Just One of Those Things" emphasizes the most famous but least understood aspect of these famous lovers' relationship. *The Letters of Héloïse and Abélard* are not the frank and passionate love letters we of the twentieth century might expect, but rather stylized epistles with a moral purpose. Specifically the published letters describe how both Héloïse and Abélard were converted to the service and spirit of God and were led away from earthly sin and passion.

That sin and passion began with Peter Abélard, a headstrong Breton whose combination of keen intellect, vanity, and insolence built strong rivalries with resentful French church leaders from his student days onward. Just shy of 40 at the time he met Héloïse, he was at the height of his success: a brilliant, wealthy teacher, attracting students from all over Europe to the Left Bank of Paris. Not as much is known about Héloïse, the beautiful, intelligent, and educated 16-year-old niece of a Notre Dame canon named Fulbert; but, hired as her tutor, Abélard found her attributes appealing and seduction easy.

By the time her uncle discovered the affair, Héloïse was pregnant. She stayed with Abélard's sister and bore a son, Astrolabe, who was raised by his aunt and later became a priest. In an effort to protect Abélard's reputation, the lovers were secretly married. Ironically, it was secrecy of another sort that ended the marriage and Abélard's career. To avoid exacerbating the already strained relations with Fulbert, Héloïse pretended to join a nunnery. Abélard traveled there secretly to meet and make love to her. But, unaware of these meetings and assuming that Abélard had merely rid himself of Héloïse, Fulbert took revenge by hiring thugs to castrate him. With the ensuing scandal, Abélard's hopes for a high position in the Church were ended, and Héloïse legitimately took religious vows.

Years later they resumed frequent contact when Abélard helped Héloïse, then an abbess, establish a nunnery at his old school, the Paraclete. It was during this time that the letters were written. All but forgotten for centuries, the story of Abélard and Héloïse was revived in the 1600s and has since become legendary. Each age has interpreted the pair for its own purposes, sometimes as ideal lovers, sometimes, as Mark Twain, castigating Abélard as a "cold seducer." In the end, though historical accuracy may have suffered, the legend has helped preserve these remarkable personalities. Their cultlike following undoubtedly inspired Lenoir to build the monument which stands here—not merely to sentimental lovers or a seducer and his victim, but rather to two important people who, through their writings, have given us an enlightened view of the Middle Ages.

DIVISION 8

Here lies **Georges Cuvier** (1769–1832), the naturalist who revolutionized zoological classification and is considered the father of comparative anatomy.

DIVISION 9

Mlle George (Margaret Josephine Weimer, 1787–1867) was an actress who, despite her strapping frame, excelled in tragic roles. During a brief affair with Napoléon, the always inventive Emperor created a special type of elastic garter for her.

Walking along Avenue Latérale du Sud, you may be startled to come across a woman kneeling with her arms outstretched, looking as if she would be more at home on the prow of a sailing ship than landlocked in Père Lachaise. The wife of sculptor **Paul Dubois** (1829–1905) posed for this monument. Dubois also created Bizet's bust in Division 68.

DIVISION 10

This section is divided equally between literature and science: **Rémy de Gourmont** (1858–1915), a writer who excelled in poetry, drama, fiction, aesthetics, grammar, and literary criticism. A mysterious facial disfigurement which appeared in his thirties and an unhappy love affair propelled him into a hermitlike existence, though he would reappear from time to time in search of romance.

Edouard Branly (1844–1940), inventor of the radio coherer, which helped make wireless telegraphy possible.

DIVISION 11

People sometimes claim to hear strains of faint music coming from Division 11. It is hardly surprising, when one considers the amount of musical talent in repose here.

Ginette Neveu (1919–1949). The brilliant career of this young violinist was cut short by an airplane crash on her

way to the United States. That crash also ended the life of her brother and accompanist, **Jean Neveu** (1918–1949). Their monument, modern yet classic in its simplicity, is an affecting remembrance.

Luigi Cherubini (1760–1842). This large tomb is noteworthy because it depicts the bust of the composer being crowned with a laurel wreath by a muse who is carved in full figure—perhaps to show eternal art honoring the achievement of ephemeral man. Cherubini's chief contribution was the manner in which his music opened up the dramatic possibilities of opera. He concentrated on presenting the psychological conflicts his characters experienced, in the process de-emphasizing musical ornamentation and prettiness. This style was best put to use in his opera *Médée* (Medea, 1797). His requiems were highly regarded in their day and are still rewarding. Cherubini served conscientiously as director of the Conservatoire from 1822 to 1842. His efforts did much to solidify its reputation and establish its future course.

Vincenzo Bellini (1801–1835). Topped by the ubiquitous lyre which decorates musicians' tombs of this period, Bellini's tomb has the titles of his greatest works inscribed on its side. He, however, was returned to Italy in 1876.

André Grétry (1741–1813), creator of over 50 operas, a witty conversationalist and favorite composer of Napoléon who, unfortunately, could never remember faces. At a reception, when Napoléon once again asked his name, the composer replied patiently, "Sire, I am still Grétry."

Finally, the monument of a world-famous musician which is still used as a private mail drop for lovers who tuck notes in its various crevices:

Tomb of the Eschylle family

FRÉDÉRIC CHOPIN *b. February 2, 1810, Zelaówa, Po-land; d. October 17, 1849, Paris. (Chopin's mother claimed he was born March 1, 1810.)* At first glance, the mournful Victorian maiden seems no different from her sisters in stone—until you get close enough to read the name at which she is pointing: Fred Chopin. Fred Chopin? It is like coming across the composer in his underwear.

Yet Chopin was always approachable, never haughty. Arriving in Paris in 1831, he had no difficulty making friends;

his circle soon included Delacroix, Heine, and Berlioz. They appreciated his musical genius and gift for mimicry, and they encouraged him in his skirmishes with Franz Liszt over dramatic vs. no-frills playing. His friends also arranged that he give lessons to young noblemen, freeing him to create the music that was already being described as "perfection itself." Through etudes, nocturnes, concertos, and polonaises, he established the piano as a solo instrument—something now taken for granted.

Two things interrupted his idyllic and productive life: the threat of another Revolution in 1848, which sent his pupils fleeing from Paris, and his increasingly poor health. Although he disliked giving concerts, for financial reasons he allowed himself to be talked into a tour in England and Scotland. Stories of his courageously playing despite blood on the keys have been exaggerated by parents to get their children to practice, but he was so weak he had to be carried back to bed after each performance.

In Paris several months later, the tuberculosis that had haunted his life finally claimed it. His deathbed scene was similar to those of classical paintings in which even beggars and small dogs hang around the fringes. At least 25 people are alleged to have crowded into his room, including priests hoping to restore his faith, artists making sketches for posterity, sopranos who sang to cheer him in his last hour, and other friends of the most popular man in Paris. The one person conspicuously absent was his former lover, George Sand, though her daughter, Solange Clésinger, stayed close to Chopin.

The statue above Chopin's tomb, representing "the genius of music sunk in grief" was created by Jean-Baptiste Clésinger, the son-in-law of George Sand, and Solange's husband. When erected it was branded mediocre, a disappointment to those who had subscribed for a memorial. Ironically, Chopin considered Clésinger a scoundrel; it was over him that Chopin and George Sand had had their final quarrel.

DIVISION 12

Here lies **François Joseph Talma** (1763–1826), actor. First to initiate the toga party (instead of playing classical roles in modern dress), he also encouraged more naturalness on the stage. Talma played right through the Revolution (with which he sympathized) and died of natural causes.

At a right angle to Talma is one of the most intriguing monuments in the cemetery, that of violinist and composer **Charles-Phillipe Lafont** (1781–1839). His tomb shows a man lying on his back holding a woman's face between his hands and has the inscription, *Ils furent émerveillés du beau voyage qui les mena jusqu'au bout de la vie.* (They marvelled at the beauty of the voyage that brought them to the end of life.)

A quite different but equally charming monument is that of **Jean Carries** (1856–1894). The statue shows the miniaturist dressed in a slouched felt hat and work clothes, holding one of his tiny figures on the palm of his hand.

Finally, a more famous artist, **Théodore Géricault** (1791–1824), who died after being thrown from a horse. Here we find the painter reclining in bed, palette and brush in hand. Is he struggling to complete a painting on his deathbed, or is he allegorically studying his life's work? Beneath him, in bas relief, is a depiction of his masterpiece *The Raft of the Medusa*.

Théodore Gericault

DIVISION 13

There are two interesting tombs in this section. The stele with what appears to be flames on the top is that of **Sophie Blanchard** (1778–1819), a foremost woman balloonist, who died ascending from the Tivoli Gardens when her balloon was ignited by a firework. Her husband, **Jean Pierre Blanchard** (1753–1809), inventor of the parachute, also died in a balloon accident, at LeHaye, France.

Slightly down the path (see map) is the charming monument of composer **Gabriel Pierné** (1862–1937), which, in art deco style, shows two women in classical dress. One is seated playing two flutes; the other stands behind her, her head sorrowfully averted from the mask of comedy which she holds in her right hand. Pierné enjoyed success as both a composer and conductor. Of his music, his songs and chamber works are especially noteworthy. They are stylishly written, utilizing clarity and lightness of form in an original, although definitely French, manner. As a conductor he generously devoted much time to performing the music of his contemporaries.

DIVISION 14

Jean Fresnel (1788–1827), who invented the compound lens for lighthouses and was one of the developers of the wave theory of light.

DIVISION 15

One of the most startling graves in Père Lachaise is that of the poet **George Rodenbach** (1855–1898). It depicts Rodenbach bursting out of his tomb, extending his arm upward to hold open the lid and proffer a rose to passersby. His frail, moustachioed face belies the fact that he was a successful trial lawyer before he turned to literature.

CHAPTER 2

PÈRE LACHAISE
Tour Two

▲　▲　▲

DIVISION 17

TWO PHILOSOPHERS SHARE this division. One, **Michel Chasles** (1793–1880), was a good mathematician and historian but a poor judge of character. Over the years he bought the "original letters" of Cleopatra, and those of Mary Magdalene to Jesus—all in French. He was publicly embarrassed when the forger was put on trial. The other savant, Auguste Comte, undoubtedly would not have made this mistake.

AUGUSTE COMTE b. *January 19, 1798, Montpellier; d. September 5, 1857, Paris.* Reflecting the hidden fears of us all, Comte specified that he was not to be buried until he was "unmistakably dead." His disciples dutifully waited three days for any signs to the contrary, then carried him to Père Lachaise. A man used to giving orders, Auguste also specified that there was to be no autopsy and no embalming, and that no "false disciples," members of his estranged wife's family, or members of the Ecole Polytechnique were to be allowed to participate.

It was typical of Comte that even in death he would be preoccupied with those who disagreed with him. If his early mentor, Saint-Simon, had been alive he would have been glad to exclude him, too, and even his parents, a doting mother and civil-servant father, didn't escape periodic excommunication.

The high regard in which Auguste was held at home and at school (he could glance at a page once and recite it backwards) gave him the confidence to pursue his ideas—and also gave him an exaggerated idea of his own infallibi-

Opposite: Wife of François Vincent Raspail

lity. After graduating from the Ecole Polytechnique, he apprenticed himself to Saint-Simon, who was more of a social activist than a systematic thinker. Although Comte eventually rechristened his teacher "Lucifer" and condemned his lack of scientific methodology, he learned much from Saint-Simon. The break came when Comte insisted on publishing *Plan of the Scientific Operations Necessary for Reorganizing Society* under his own name, and Saint-Simon wrote a preface criticizing the work as sketchy and incomplete.

During this time he had persuaded Caroline Massin, a young prostitute, to live with him before they married. They did wed eventually and stayed together 17 years, during which she nursed him through a mental breakdown and a suicide attempt. He reciprocated with physical attacks which made her often flee for her life. Still, Caroline was no doormat; she finally left when she had had enough, though he insisted she stay and look after him until his best-known work, *Cours de Philosophie Positive* (Positive Philosophy, 1830–1842), was completed.

This cornerstone of his philosophical work proposed that everything—including human behavior—could be known by scientific observation. He devised a hierarchy that rose from mathematics through astronomy, physics, chemistry, and biology to sociology, in which each existed to shed light on the discipline above it. Comte also postulat-

(A) François Raspail
(B) Jean Champollion
(C) Auguste Comte
(D) Samuel Hahnemann
(E) Mlle. Raucourt
(F) Gustave Doré
(G) General Junot
(H) Jean Auguste Ingres
(I) René Lalique
(J) Honoré Daumier
(K) Camille Corot
(M) Joseph Louis Gay-Lussac
(N) Gabrielle Russier
(P) Molière
 Jean La Fontaine

(Q) Alphonse Daudet
(R) Comte de Saint-Simon
(S) General Foy
 Anna Bibesco
(T) Beaumarchais
(U) Marshall Masséna
(V) Jean Anthelme Brillat-Savarin
(W) David d'Angers
(X) Le Père Enfantin
(Y) Greuffülhe family
(Z) Admiral William Sidney Smith
(a) Emma Valadon
(b) Nadar (Tournachon)
(c) Comte Lavalette
(d) Talleyrand

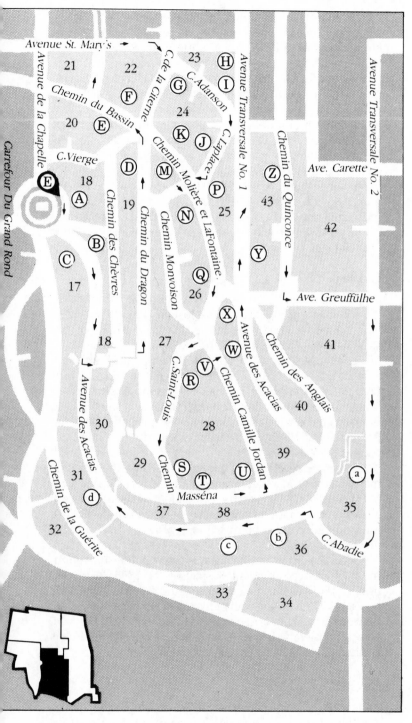

ed that mankind had begun with theological explanations, gone on to metaphysical reasoning (i.e. that stars moved in circles because a circle was the most perfect figure), and finally reached the correct idea of cause and effect.

In later life, after his written attacks on L'Ecole Polytechnique had caused its administrators to drop his teaching contract, Auguste worked to develop his Religion of Humanity. Much of it deified a young woman with whom he had fallen in love, Clotilde de Vaux. Fortunately for his theory, she died of tuberculosis a year after they met, before his usual disillusionment could set in.

His idealization of Clotilde helped to humanize the Father of Sociology, who loved mankind but couldn't stand its individual parts, who symbolically ate a crust of bread each evening for dessert but could not tolerate an opinion different from his own.

DIVISION 18

Walking down the Avenue des Acacias, we come first to the tomb of phrenologist **Franz Joseph Gall** (1758–1828), who claimed he had located the "hump of crime" on the skull of man. His bust was erected by and is maintained under the auspices of the British Phrenological Society.

Farther down, also on the right, is the stele to **Jean François Champollion** (1790–1832), Napoléon's brilliant officer who spoke nine Oriental languages. In 1821 he discovered the key to decoding hieroglyphics by use of the Rosetta Stone, discovered earlier during the Egyptian campaign (1799).

Just before reaching the center circle is the huge family mausoleum of Marshall **François Christophe Kellermann** (1735–1820), best known as commander of the army of the Moselle and victor of the battle of Valmy in 1792. The monument, propped up by wooden planks, is in a sad state of deterioration.

Inside the circle, on the right, is the very unusual monument of **François Vincent Raspail** (1794–1878), a revolutionary who was imprisoned during the revolutions of 1830 and 1848. High on the wall of his tomb is a barred window. Beneath it, with her arm extended so her hand can reach in, is the completely shrouded figure of his wife. The statue is at once graceful, mysterious, and sorrowful.

DIVISION 19

Located on the Chemin des Chêvres not far to the right of the stairs leading to Demidoff's monument, are two striking tombs of otherwise unknown families. The **d'Herbe** family tomb has a beautiful mosaic of a woman leaning on a cane and standing in a colorful garden. Just to its right is the elaborate art nouveau tomb of the **Guêts**. Its outer two pillars are stylised figures. Under the left is the question *Unde Venis?* (From whence do you come?); under the right, *Quo Vadis?* (Where are you going?).

Proceeding left to the stairs one can look up at the imposing monument dedicated to the Russian princess **Elizabeth Demidoff**, who died in 1818. This huge temple carries with it the legend that a reward of two million rubles awaits the person who can stay one year within its confines. The temple is decorated with otter and wolf heads and, more understandably, with miners' hammers—the family's fortune came from its gold, silver, and copper mines. Inside, the princess rests in a sarcophogus of white marble.

To the left along the Chemin du Dragon is the tomb of **Geoffrey Saint-Hilaire** (1772–1844), who did brilliant work in comparative anatomy and founded the zoo in the Paris Botanical Gardens. His stele is decorated by two grateful whooping cranes.

In the other direction, past Mausolée Demidoff, are the tombs of two contrasting doctors: that of **Samuel Hahnemann** (1755–1853), father of immunology, whose large rose granite monument and bust were erected by a grateful international following; and that of **Dr. Joseph Ignace Guillotin** (1738–1814), who adapted the guillotine from an earlier Scottish device with the humanitarian aim of stopping more brutal kinds of executions. Before its use he had been a leading society doctor in Paris; after its initiation his practice fell apart.

DIVISION 20

Françoise Raucourt (1756–1815), a stately, deep-voiced actress whose offstage affairs with both men and women scandalized the public. It was because she was an actress, however, that the Church attempted to deny her a Catholic burial. But this time the crowds, tired of that particular prejudice, forced open the doors of St. Roch and carried her coffin inside, where it was finally, if reluctantly, blessed.

DIVISION 22

Gustave Doré (1833–1883), a well-known illustrator whose dramatic and macabre style illuminated such works as Dante's *Inferno* and Milton's *Paradise Lost*.

DIVISION 23

As might be expected, the grave of **René Lalique** (1860–

1945), the famous glassmaker, has a sample of his work: a crucifixion scene etched in glass.

The other monument of note in this section is of **Jean Auguste Ingres** (1780–1867), a grand old man of the French neoclassical school and darling of the Salon. So busy painting was he that both his marriages, arranged by friends, were to women he had never met. And both were as successful as his art.

DIVISION 24

Except for **Andoche Junot** (1771–1813), all the noted inhabitants here are artists. Junot, one of Napoléon's most interesting generals, collected fine editions, employed the famous chef Carême, and called his half-Abyssinian son Othello. He also, in a fit of despair at being exiled, threw himself from a window in Illyria.

The prints of the first artist here, **Honoré Daumier**

(1808–1879), are often reprinted in America today. Daumier's satirical cartoons of Louis-Philippe's reign first brought him fame in Paris—and then six months in jail. He also satirized lawyers and the bourgeoisie and did more serious drawings on the problems of the poor. His tomb, a flat slab which has slid off its foundations, is depressingly uncared for.

In better condition is the large family bed of the painter Corot, which features a bust of the artist atop a long wall listing the names of his entire family.

Jean-Baptiste-Camille Corot

JEAN-BAPTISTE-CAMILLE COROT *b. July 16, 1796, Paris; d. February 22, 1875, Paris.* The bust of Corot is a handsome one, but it makes him look colder and more formal than he actually was. "Père Corot" was eminently approachable and gave so freely of his time and resources that he was nicknamed the St. Vincent de Paul of Painting; in later years, having no children of his own, he especially enjoyed his paternal relationship to younger artists.

Unlike artists such as David, Corot was not a man of ideas. He rarely read a book, never the newspaper, and did not conceive of paintings as needing meanings. He had no interest in what lay beneath the surface, preferring to accept what he saw both in painting and in life. Corot was like a kindly old bachelor uncle whose life is an open, though not very interesting, book.

From an early age Corot wanted to study art, but his father, a well-to-do cloth merchant, wouldn't hear of it. It was not until Camille had done undistinguished work in school and failed abysmally at business that his father finally allowed him, at 26, to study painting. (His father never thought much of the profession; when Camille was given the Legion of Honor in 1846, M. Corot, Sr. refused to believe it, thinking initially that the award must have been meant for himself.)

In his own words, Corot was married to Art. But, like many marriages, this one had a public and a private face. His official paintings, those which he did to please the Salon, had titles such as *Hagar in the Wilderness* and *Macbeth and the Witches*. Such paintings, to which he often added a few figures to make them "classical," did not always succeed.

His private paintings, which have interested posterity ever since, show the work that he did for love. A number of them anticipate the impressionists in their freshness of vision and technique. He would have been surprised to learn that he helped initiate a movement. As he sometimes commented, "I have only a little flute but I try to play the right note."

DIVISION 25

Although neither La Fontaine nor Molière were originally buried here, chances are they would have been pleased by the change. Born only a year apart, they were close friends. La Fontaine's tomb has characters from his fables in bronze on its sides. Molière's is a simple stone canopy.

JEAN LA FONTAINE *b. July 8, 1621, Chateau de Thierry; d. April 13, 1695, Paris.* Like the best of the animals he wrote about, La Fontaine was good-hearted, sensuous, and utterly without guile. He was a terrible husband and father but was reputed to be a good friend. Best known for his fables, he told them with wit and narrative skill, investing the animals with human traits and treating them sympathetically. It was an identification he never lost.

La Fontaine's father, whose title was Master of Water and Forests for the King, encouraged in him a love of poetry, but he did not approve of Jean's lighthearted amours. In 1647 when the son was 26, his father arranged Jean's marriage to 15-year-old Marie Héricart. They were compatible—both enjoyed literature, spending money, and having love affairs—but neither was practical enough to run a home. Jean rarely saw their one son, Charles. (Passing Charles as an adult, his father frowned, "I think I have seen that young man before.")

In 1658 Jean and Marie finally separated, and La Fontaine fell into a pattern of residing in the homes of wealthy patrons. He became close friends with Racine, Molière, and Boileau, and when the four dined together there were penalties for using clichés and affectations, and for not accepting the criticism of the group. By then he was established as a poet and storyteller. His fables were well-received and his tales, drawn from early Italian stories, were charming and ribald to the point where the king objected—unsuccessfully—to Jean's election to the Académie Française in 1683.

In the end it was La Fontaine himself who decided to set his moral house in order. His housekeeper begged his proselytizers, "Do not torment him, he is more stupid than wicked. God would never have the courage to damn him!" One, the Abbé Poujet, began giving him religious instruction. At least once, when the Abbé was not sure of the morality of La Fontaine's newly completed comedy, he submitted it to a group of authorities who, of course, condemned it. La Fontaine obediently threw his only copy into the fire.

From then on, redemption was his only goal. In one of the last prayers he wrote before he died, still identifying with animals, he implored God to "Separate me from the goats."

MOLIÈRE (Jean Louis Poquelin) *b. 1622, Paris; d. 1673, Paris.* Molière, accustomed to touring the countryside to drum up interest in his plays, would have understood the reasons for transferring his remains to the struggling new attraction, Père Lachaise. He might even have been pleased with the attention, since his original burial 144 years earlier had been clandestine. Because actors were denied a Christian burial, it had taken the influence of Louis XIV to have him interred at St. Eustache—and only on the condition that it be done at night, without a ceremony.

Jean Louis Poquelin knew of such prejudices, of course, when he chose the theater over his inherited job entitled Rugseller to the King. But at 19 he met actress Madeleine Béjart and quickly formed a personal and professional relationship with her. (Twenty-one years later he would wed Armande Béjart, Madeleine's illegitimate child, giving rise to the calumny that he was marrying his own daughter.)

But before that happened, he had to transform mannered Italian comedy with its set comic routines, stock situations, and slapstick gags into plays with philosophic meanings and emotional validity. Modern viewers of *The Misanthrope*, *Tartuffe*, and *A School for Wives* may find his plays over-stylized, with characters just missing and misunderstanding each other, and a too-abundant use of disguises and props. Nevertheless the plays are still being produced.

Molière sought to mirror the foibles of his society rather than attack them, but by presenting things as they were he made a number of enemies anyway. Nobles who promoted religious teachings to assert their rule, stiffly conventional bourgeoisie, and the Church herself found ample cause for outrage. Molière, however, was canny enough to keep from offending King Louis and managed to stage his plays at Versailles.

His last play was *The Imaginary Invalid*, in which players twice feign death to get a reaction from other players. He himself fell ill onstage and died, at 51, in the middle of that play's fourth performance. There is no evidence that he came back to life, even temporarily, to see what kind of effect he had made.

DIVISION 26

Joseph Louis Gay-Lussac (1778–1850), the scientist who developed the law of volumes which states that the ratio of gases combined remains the same in the product. Gay-Lussac also made several balloon ascents as high as twenty-three thousand feet to discover the composition of air at high altitudes and to measure the pull of the earth's magnetic field.

Alphonse Daudet (1840–1897). Although a famous author in his time, Daudet has fallen into obscurity in the twentieth century, a fact that his tomb rather eerily predicts. You must walk around to the back of the **Allard** and **Daudet** family mausoleum to find his portrait sculpted into one corner. Alphonse's eyes are averted, as if accepting his fate and below his cameo are listed his works, including novels *Le Petit Chose* (The Little Good-for-Nothing, 1868), *Jack* (1876), *Le Nabab* (The Nabob, 1877) and *L'Immortel* (The Immortal, 1888).

Nearby is also **Gabrielle Russier** (1937–1969), quietly buried in her family's mausoleum, a victim of the 1960s. It was a time of campus protests, the Beatles, and "Make love, not war" slogans, a time when anything seemed possible; and Gabrielle, a sheltered academic and divorced mother of young twins, fell desperately in love with one of her students, Christian, aged 18. He happily returned her affection, but the new freedoms of the sixties proved illusory. His parents lodged a complaint, and she was convicted of "detouring a minor" (custodial interference). In an unusually punitive gesture, Gabrielle was threatened with a long jail term. Unable to face it, she asphixiated herself instead.

DIVISION 27

General **Joseph Léopold Hugo** (1773–1828), father of Victor, is buried here along with other family members. A career officer, he traveled constantly with Napoléon's army and did some writing on military subjects. Victor Hugo is buried in the Panthéon.

DIVISION 28

To tour this heavily laden section, it is best to start on Chemin Camille Jordan, at the simple tomb of the gastronome and judge, **Jean-Anthèlme Brillat-Savarin** (1755–1826). Although his injunctions barring dogs, cats, flowers, small children, and women wearing perfume from the dining room of the true gourmand might have offended some, his book *La Physiologie du Goût* (The Physiology of Taste, 1825) is a witty and timeless classic.

Rounding the corner, we find the monuments of marshalls **André Masséna** (1758–1817) and **Pierre-François-Joseph Lefèbvre** (1755–1820), both career officers in the French army and highly decorated for their pains. When a friend complained about the honors and income with which they had retired, Lefèbvre told him, "Well, you can have it all for what we paid. We'll go down into the garden, I will fire at you 60 times and then, if you are not killed, everything will be yours."

A little farther down is the monument of one of the most colorful inhabitants of Père Lachaise:

BEAUMARCHAIS (Pierre Auguste Caron) *b. January 24, 1732, Paris; d. May 18, 1799, Paris.* Those familiar with the baroque complications of Beaumarchais' *The Barber of Seville* and *The Marriage of Figaro* may be surprised to find that the author's life was an even more intricate web of names, occupations, affairs, and diversions. In his life he was a playwright, musician, satirist, rebel, inventor, spy, and scamp, but above all he was a moving force in the affairs of France and America.

Starting as a watchmaker's son, Paul Auguste Caron was known as "fils Caron" (son of Caron). By the age of 20 he had invented an escapement which is still in use today. So fine was his idea that the royal watchmaker stole it. So bold was fils Caron that the commoner challenged for credit and won.

He also won the attention of Mme Madeline Francquet, the young wife of the aging comptroller for the royal court. They pursued an affair, and when her husband died they married. Their bliss quickly soured, ending when the harping wife joined the heavenly band a mere ten months after the marriage, but not before fils Caron took the name Beaumarchais, after his wife's estate. In becoming titled he also had to declare himself a Catholic, thus abjuring his Protestant background. And so by his mid-twenties he had changed his name, religion, and class standing.

He further ingratiated himself in the royal court with his musical talents and then moved ahead through a series of appointments and close friendships with the wealthy and powerful. Beaumarchais' love life kept apace. He had another affair, followed again by marriage after the husband's death, only this time there was a son. This marriage was far happier, but luck did not follow, for his wife died after two years and his son after four.

Beaumarchais next became embroiled in a suit with unscrupulous but powerful figures in the government, resulting in great financial distress and a public reprimand which denied him his civil rights. More importantly, however, he became a public hero. His four memoirs published in his defense detailed governmental corruption; their style—brazen, satirical, yet deadly serious—gathered him much admiration, including that of Voltaire and, oddly, Louis XV, who sought out his services to squelch the slanderous pamphlets being published in England about the French royal family. Accomplishing this under the name of M. de Ronac (anagrams, anybody?) he gained further prestige and influence with the crown, although he remained without his civil rights.

With the crowning of Louis XVI, his de facto importance increased to the point where he was second to none, a position he used with great skill in getting the government to aid American colonies in their revolution. Beaumarchais badgered the King into an active role, decried the support of slavery, and furnished supplies to the colonies through a phony trading company which he organized and partly financed. He also sent officers to help the American army and armed his ships so they could fight the British navy. The colonies could not have hoped for a more important or influential ally than they found in Beaumarchais.

His reputation today rests primarily on his plays. Thinly disguised as comedies, they were in reality social satires and potent political statements which many in power sought to ban. How did he get them performed? Through his tenacity and brazen charm, the same qualities to be found in the plays' hero, Figaro (fils Caron). Their message was not missed, and their fame quickly spread. *The Barber of Seville* was set to music by Rossini and *The Marriage of Figaro* by Mozart. Beaumarchais was all but stone deaf by the time he saw Mozart's masterpiece performed.

It is ironic that Figaro the character may now be more famous than his author, but the two shared so many traits we can feel certain we are looking at one person.

Continuing on the Chemin Massena, we find one of the most poignant, if unrealistic, outcries against dying in the cemetery, that of **Anna Bibesco, Comtesse de Noailles** (1876–1933). Inside the large, domed family edifice, decorated with lions and coats of arms, her photo rests on the floor attended by two sorrowing angels. Its inscription laments, "Alas, I am not fated to be dead."

At the fork is an impressive monument to French general **Maximilien Foy** (1755–1825), who fought in the Napoléonic Wars. Although conscientious, he repeatedly erred on the battlefield. His brigade was regularly surprised or routed. While crucial areas were being lost, he sent men into unimportant battles elsewhere and was himself wounded 15 times. Foy did better in peacetime as a popular liberal deputy (an elected official), whose credo was "freedom of the individual and freedom of the press"—no empty issue in those days.

In contrast to Foy's monument, the tomb of **Claude-Henri Rouvroy, Comte de Saint-Simon** (1760–1825) is very plain, in keeping with his later teachings. As a young man he came to America and fought in the Revolutionary War on the side of the colonies, then returned to France and amassed a fortune in real estate. He used this to set up laboratories for scientists and took a vow of poverty himself. His philosophy, Saint-Simonism, which combined socialism and scientific progress with the teachings of Jesus, spread throughout Europe after his death.

DIVISION 29

In this section are five lesser known, but no less fascinating, personalities.

Pierre Paul Prud'hon (1758–1823) and his mistress, **Constance Mayer** (1782–1821). Both painters, their work has been somewhat overshadowed by her tragic end. When the incapacitated Mme Prud'hon was finally dying, Constance (who had raised Prud'hon's five children) asked him if he would ever marry again. "No, never," Prud'hon answered emphatically, perhaps not realizing she was proposing to him. His rejection confirmed her worst fears that, nearing 40, her beauty had faded, and she slashed her throat with his razor. He tried vainly to save her life but failed. After that he lost his own enthusiasm for living.

Marshall **Michel Ney** (1769–1815) who meteored through the system to become a general, a marshall, a prince, and finally a peer under Louis XVIII. Ungratefully, he rallied to Napoléon during the Hundred Days, was tried by the Chamber of Peers and shot for treason. His tomb is a large circular area of warheads linked by chains, with a bas relief of Ney in the center.

Claude Chappe (1763–1805), inventor of a telegraph using visual semaphore signals, which was used on rooftops all over Paris to relay signals from the front during times of war. His monument is easy to spot because of the replica of his creation on its top.

Benjamin Constant (1767–1830) who, despite his name, couldn't make up his mind. After his mother died the brilliant boy was raised by a series of sadistic and incompetent tutors who greatly affected his outlook. His novel *Adolphe* (1816) was enthusiastically received, but in his private life he vacillated for 16 years between staying with his tempestuous lover Germaine de Staël, herself a writer, or breaking the relationship off. (He actually had been married several months before he dared admit it to Mme de Staël.)

Constant also attacked Napoléon in the press until the Emperor offered him a writing job, which Constant quickly accepted. Yet after Waterloo he held fast to his liberal beliefs, and his funeral was the occasion for a great demonstration among Parisians.

DIVISION 30

Mlle Duchesnois (Catherine Joséphine Rafien, 1777–1835), an unusually plain actress who was further handicapped by a past which included kitchen work, prostitution, and a horsetrading husband. Fortunately she had great acting ability and an excellent figure, which she liked to reveal.

DIVISION 31

Occupying an entire area himself, is one of the most enigmatic figures of the cemetery, **Charles Maurice Talleyrand-Périgord** (1754–1838). Not one for letting his religious vows or his position as Bishop of Autun cramp his style, Talleyrand gave private instruction to the beauties of his day. Madame de Staël came under his spell as did Adele de Souza, who produced his son Charles de Flahaut, father of the Duc de Morny. The painter Eugène Delacroix was also alleged to have been born on the wrong side of Talleyrand's blanket.

But Talleyrand's real brilliance shone in the political power he wielded behind the scenes. After initially siding with the revolutionaries in 1879, he took refuge in England and America when the guillotine became popular. Talleyrand had a remarkable ability for riding out the storms of politics. He supported the return of the Bourbons and, as Louis XVIII's minister, negotiated the Treaty of Paris in 1814, triumphing at the Congress of Vienna. Under Louis-Philippe he was made ambassador to England. At his best, he helped to stabilize both Europe, and France's political position in Europe. At his worst, he spun endless intrigues which condemned some men to their deaths.

His own death came naturally at 84. But after his funeral, when the carriage driver asked which road to take, his grandson Auguste de Morny swore that he heard a voice from within the coffin groan, "The road to hell!"

DIVISION 35

The small stone sepulchure of **Emma Valadon** (1837–1913) and her two children belies her boisterous career as the café singer "Thérésa." Plump, big-mouthed, racy, she endeared herself to music hall society with such favorites as "La Femme Barbue" (The Bearded Lady) before retiring to her farm in Normandy at 56. Degas commented, "She opens her big mouth and out comes a voice that is the most roughly, the most delicately, the most wittily tender that exists. With soul, with taste. Where can one find anything better?"

DIVISION 36

Hidden behind two overgrown shrubs which are planted in its base is the tomb of the photographer and satirist **Nadar** (Gaspard-Felix Tournachon, 1820–1910), who pioneered in aerial photography and became the leading photographer of the Catacombs, documenting its burial sites for posterity.

A little farther down Avenue des Acacias is the entertaining monument of **Comte Lavalette** who died in 1839. Condemned to death for his continuing loyalty to Napoléon I after the failure of the Hundred Days in 1815, he escaped by dressing in his wife's clothing—as shown in the bas relief on the tomb.

DIVISION 37

Despite his fine statue, **Général Gobert**, shown sliding off his horse at the moment of death (1808) does not appear in the history books. The battles he fought in, listed around the base—Guadalupe, Egypt, and Famars, give some explanation of why he is crushing an Indian under his horse's hooves. The statue is considered one of David d'Angers' finest.

A little farther up the path is the stele of **Albert Winsor** (1763–1830), topped with a torch to commemorate his introducing street lamps to Paris. Before 1829, in the City of Lights Parisians were given candles and ordered to keep them lit in second-floor windows.

Also in this section is the chapel of **Nicolas Frochot**, the urban planner who helped create Père Lachaise and facilitated its purchase.

DIVISION 39

Under a bust that looks like Father Christmas lies **Barthelemy-Prosper Enfantin** (Le Père, 1796–1864), a disciple of Saint-Simon, who strongly promoted his teacher's writings and founded a socialist community at Menilmontant. The softened appearance of the stone gives the deceased a strong yet serene countenance.

This section also contains the relatively plain tomb of **Pierre-Jean David d'Angers** (1788–1856), the man responsible for more funerary sculpture in Père Lachaise and Montparnasse than anyone else.

DIVISION 43

In this section, along Avenue Transversale No. 1, is the chapel of the **Greffülhe** family erected in 1815. Looking like a small church with round stained-glass windows, two steeples in front, and a cross on top, it signaled a change from single-occupancy sites to the tomb as a family affair. Or, more symbolically, it demonstrated a reduced interest in the individual soul, concomitant with a growing need to eternally honor the family—a concession to group vanity. Its distinction lies in its being the first family tomb in Paris.

By walking back to the next aisle and turning left, you can locate one of the few monuments in Père Lachaise written in English, that of **Sir Admiral William Sidney Smith** (1764–1840). The coffin-shaped monument also contains his wife, **Caroline Mary** (1764–1826) and has a bronze bas relief of his profile which does not completely express his quick temper and bon vivant charm. Smith was a British admiral, a holder of the Grand Cross of Order of the Bath, who fought in the French Revolutionary and Napoléonic Wars—for England. Yet his heart belonged to Paris, and after the wars ended he settled here permanently.

Barthélémy-Prosper Enfantin

CHAPTER 3

PÈRE LACHAISE
Tour Three

▲   ▲   ▲

DIVISION 44

EVEN BEFORE YOU reach the next tomb, you will assume from the groups of people gathered around and masses of flowers surrounding it that it belongs to someone important. You may be surprised, then, to find that the simple bronze bust in the stone alcove is that of a man who isn't in any of the standard biographical dictionaries:

ALLAN KARDEC (a.k.a. Léon Rivail) *b. 1804, Lyons; d. 1869, Paris.* If a vote had been taken on who was least likely to become the new leader of spiritualism, Léon Rivail could have won hands down. An unimaginative, hard-working drone, he came to Paris at 20 after publishing a book on mathematical theory. As a professor at the Academy of Paris, he published works on education and French grammar, subjects which could be expounded on and proved.

When Rivail first heard of the spiritualism which had sprung to life in Hydesville, New York, aided by levitating tables and ghostly knockings, he was skeptical, replying in unimaginative fashion, "I'll believe it when I see it." He was not particularly interested, but he finally went to a seance and became convinced that there was "something there." He investigated it further and put down his findings in *The Book of Spirits*, becoming the infant movement's leading spokesman.

Kardec differentiated his own theory from spiritualism, calling it spiritism, and saw it as the manifestation of things from the invisible world. Even so, he was selective in what he reported that the spirits were telling him, noting that, "There is no shortage of writers in the invisible world, but,

Opposite: Marie d'Agoult (Daniel Stern)

as on Earth, the good ones are rare."

Allan Kardec (whose new name was chosen for him by the spirits) was initially buried at Montmartre, then moved to Père Lachise. His remains are under a copy of a bust by Charles-Romain Capellaro (the original is at the headquarters of *The Review of Spiritism* which Kardec also founded). Picture-taking of the grave is forbidden, and at any time of day there are enough of his followers around to enforce the rule. The other injunction, not to leave flowers when there is no room, appears to be ignored.

By contrast with Kardec, the other important resident of this area, though revered during her lifetime, is now all but forgotten under a plain stone canopy.

SARAH BERNHARDT *b. October 22 or 23, 1844, Paris; d. March 26, 1923, Paris.* Despite her anglicized name, Sarah Bernhardt was French, born in Paris in 1884, the illegitimate daughter of a milliner-turned-courtesan and a visiting law student. Her mother, whose friends later included Alexandre Dumas and the Duc de Morny (he was the one who first suggested that Sarah become an actress), had little interest in a small child. Sarah was farmed out to various nurses and eventually to a convent at Versailles where, though Jewish, she vowed to become a nun.

Her piety lasted until she returned to Paris and dedicated

herself instead to the theater. Extremely slender her entire life, she loved acting and especially playing boys' roles. By the end of her career she had starred in 125 plays, as well as 22 revivals of her specialty, *La Dame aux Camélias*. Well into her seventies Bernhardt toured England, Europe, and America to wild acclaim.

Her life closely resembled the melodramas in which she acted. At 20 she gave birth to her only child, Maurice, whom she adored—and whose financial irresponsibility plagued her for the rest of her life. Committed to her career, she was expelled from the Comédie Française for slapping another actress and could not get reinstated for 10 years. Her one brief marriage was to a man 11 years her junior, Jacques Damala, a morphine addict who billed her for his gifts to other women. Her younger sister, Jeanne, died of morphine addiction as well, and the other sister, Regina, of tuberculosis while still a teenager. Finally, Sarah herself had a gangrenous leg amputated when she was 70.

Sarah approached the uncertainty of her life with an amazing joie de vivre. When not on stage, she ascended in hot air balloons, hunted alligators, and kept wild animals—lynx, baby tigers and lions—in her home. Though supremely egotistical—she preferred that the actresses she shared the stage with be of mediocre ability—she was never stuffy. The story is told of how she inadvertently seated a banker next to his ex-wife at a dinner party. Realizing it, she said cheerfully, "You two have just been divorced, haven't you? What a lot you must have to tell each other!"

It is true that she always slept with a coffin in her room. She had done so since adolescence when, diagnosed as terminally consumptive, she persuaded her mother to buy her one so she could get used to sleeping in it. But someone less interested in death could hardly be imagined. She took the loss of her leg admirably and was rehearsing for a new play when she collapsed at 78, dying of uremia on March 26, 1923.

Always the consummate actress, Sarah would have enjoyed the fanfare of her funeral and the way the cortege paused dramatically in front of the Theatre Sarah Bernhardt before continuing to her final engagement at Père Lachaise.

DIVISION 46

Across from Allan Kardec is sculptress **Noémie Rouvier** (1832–1888), who adopted the pseudonym Claude Vignon from a seventeenth-century male painter. She designed her own bust and monument, showing the tools of her trade—a hammer and chisel.

DIVISION 48

A number of comments, some of them unkind, have
been made about the towering monument of diplomat
Félix de Beaujour. Rising 143 feet into the air, it is the
erection of a man who was relatively unimportant in his
lifetime. We can only guess at the cause for this inflated
grandeur: compensation? a high opinion of himself? or the
revenge of the impotent? What is certain, however, is that
this is not a man at rest.

Dwarfed by Beaujour, but an impressive monument of a completely different sort is that built to honor 16-year-old **Marie-Emilie Diaz-Santos** (1811–1827). Its wistful beauty shows, in half-relief, the Angel of Death spiriting Marie-Emilie away.

Finally, the monument of an author who wrote about Père Lachaise Cemetery before coming to take its rest cure himself:

HONORÉ DE BALZAC *b. May 20, 1799, Tours; d. August 18, 1850, Paris.* Many people's strivings for fame and fortune seem compensatorily linked to perceived or actual maternal neglect. The life of Balzac is a good example. Spending 9 of his first 14 years away from home, Balzac saw little of his parents, for they visited rarely. It was his mother's neglect, however, that he felt most keenly, declaring in later life that he had had no mother. He was what his biographer, André Maurois, called a "bastard of the imagination."

No matter how subconscious his motives, compensation and revenge fit in nicely with Balzac's choice of a first love, Laure de Berny, a woman his mother's age. Needless to say, Madame Mère disapproved, and the long-standing liason did nothing to improve mother-son relations. Their relationship remained cool and distant until Balzac's death. Madame Mère outlived her son by four years.

The paternal influence took another course. Atheist, social reformer, and political pamphleteer, Balzac's father was given to passionate outbursts and often displayed an irreverent sense of humor. Deeply influenced by these traits, Balzac combined them with his eclectic readings in an effort to form a world view, an all-encompassing philosophy of life. His long series of novels, *The Human Comedy*, expresses this overview by detailing the intricate, multi-layered aspects of individuals and society.

True comedy is at its base serious, and this was Balzac's approach. His characters were allowed foibles without judgment, for Balzac was neither a cynic nor a moralist. Yet neither was he an optimist, supplying his readers with happy endings. He created a grand canvas of life, vivid in light and color but sombre in mood.

Throughout his life Balzac strived for love, fame, and fortune. Overweight and brutish in appearance, he overcame these deficiencies with his intelligence and exuberance and had love affairs with a series of beautiful women, most of them married. Fame came more slowly, for his novels achieved only slow acceptance. Frequently living beyond his means, he was beleaguered by financial problems until his marriage in 1850.

Honoré de Balzac

Balzac's life was one of extremes: love, exuberance, and sympathy balanced uneasily against vanity, overindulgence, and deceit. What he couldn't achieve in life he vicariously experienced through his fictional characters: looks, wealth, power, a happy childhood.

Death came only five months after his marriage to Eveline Hanski, a wealthy Polish countess with whom he had been in love for 16 years. The marriage was the fulfillment of some of his dreams, for he had gained love and wealth.

Ⓐ Sarah Bernhardt
Ⓑ Allan Kardec
Ⓒ Noémie Rouvier
Ⓓ Eugène Delacroix
Ⓔ Gérard de Nerval
Ⓕ Honoré Balzac
Ⓖ Merleau-Ponty
Ⓗ Crocé-Spinelli
Ⓙ Georges Seurat

Ⓚ Raymond Radiguet
Ⓜ Georges Bizet
   Georges Enesco
Ⓝ Marie d'Agoult
Ⓞ Duc de Morny
Ⓟ Cino del Duca
Ⓠ Louis David
Ⓡ Adolphe Thiers

PÈRE LACHAISE: Tour Three

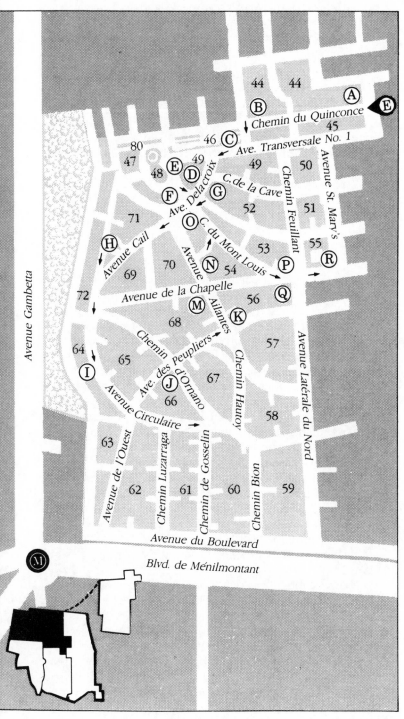

But his heart, long weak, grew worse, and his body deteriorated. With great plans for many more volumes of his series, he died at the age of 51. A more vibrant character in the human comedy cannot be imagined.

DIVISION 49

Across from Balzac is the simple stele of poet **Gérard de Nerval** (1808–1855) who, on his way home to his aunt's late one evening, hanged himself from a lamppost. Even in his madness he remained a symbolist, choosing the corner of Slaughter Street and Impasse.

If you walk directly behind de Nerval to the opposite road, you will come to the monument of an artist of calmer temperament and happier outcome.

EUGÈNE DELACROIX b. *April 26, 1798, Charenton-Saint-Maurice; d. August 13, 1863, Paris.* Eugène Delacroix, though not well known in America, was a happy man and a great artist. His work was a watershed in European art for its classically crafted yet passionate subjects. His most famous painting is probably *Liberty Leading the People*, done in 1831, which shows a robust young woman, dress pulled carelessly below her breasts, brandishing the revolutionary tricolor and stepping over the bodies of the dead.

Delacroix was dark-haired with striking, well-formed features; he had numerous mistresses but never married. Like Degas he was afraid of losing his liberty, of diluting his art with mundane responsibilities. Though he rhapsodized, "A wife who comes up to one's standards is the best thing of all," he never found one for himself.

Instead Eugène had a number of close friends, including Chopin and George Sand. He used the people he knew as subjects, flooding Paris with his vividly colored paintings. Trips to England and Morocco had great influence on his art. His painting *Jewish Wedding in Morocco* was particularly admired by the generation of artists coming behind him.

Unlike some of his contemporaries, Delacroix never became bitter or burned out. At 59 he wrote that he wished he could stay at that age, enjoying a mind that had grown "genuinely reasonable." At 62, when he was busily decorating the walls of a chapel at St. Sulpice, he exclaimed in his journal, "What a good life! A blessed compensation for all that has gone with my youth!" His pretty mistresses had been replaced by a curmudgeon of a housekeeper who guarded him against intrusions and seemed to suit him just as well.

Unfortunately, Delacroix had only two more years of enjoyment before succumbing to an old ailment, tubercular laryngitis. But he died a happy man.

DIVISION 52

Philosopher **Maurice Merleau-Ponty** (1908–1961), a proponent of phenomenology. Though he believed in the primacy of the physical world in understanding what is real, he also acknowledged a world that transcends our consciousness. As a professor of philosophy at the Sorbonne he was a colleague of Sartre, though they were never personally or professionally close.

DIVISION 53

Cino del Duca (1900–1967), movie producer, magazine publisher, and racehorse owner. The dramatic sculpting by Messina shows Mary supporting the body of Jesus after his removal from the cross.

DIVISION 54

Two fascinating contemporaries share this division. **Marie d'Agoult** (1805–1876) wrote novels as Daniel Stern. On her tomb a small head of Goethe, one of her lovers, hovers in the background with a worried expression. Her best-known liason was with Franz Liszt. One of their three children, Cosima, married composer Richard Wagner.

Then, in a mausoleum fit for royalty, lies:

AUGUSTE DE MORNY *b. ca. September 15, 1811, Saint Maurice-en-Valois; d. March 10, 1864, Paris.* Perhaps the most interesting things about the Duc de Morny are the circumstances around his birth and his death. His mother, Queen Hortense of Holland and wife of Napoléon's brother Louis, hid out during the pregnancy, pretending to have lumbago, and immediately gave her son to someone else. His "parentage" was purchased from a Prussian army kitchen worker, who later tried to blackmail the queen for more money. But by then Auguste's father, Charles de Flahaut, was pleased to acknowledge paternity. After all, he himself was the illegitmate son of Talleyrand.

Auguste grew up spoiled and insecure in his maternal grandmother's home, encouraged by her in his drive for wealth and power. He soon saw that it was in his best interests to forget the inequity of his circumstances and promote his half brother, Louis Napoléon, for emperor; he did so by intimidating voters. He was shrewd in business investments but best known as a royal adviser, though his kinship with Louis Napoléon was never openly acknowledged.

In a personality of questionable traits, de Morny's saving grace was his sense of humor. When one of the Rothschilds came to see him about a business deal, Auguste casually offered him a chair.

His guest drew himself up. "But I am a Rothschild!"

"Well, then, have two chairs."

By the time he had married, settled down into a routine, and fathered four children, he was dying. Perhaps because of previous hypochondriacal tendencies, he could not get anyone to believe it. Yellowed and weak with recurring stomach pain, he finally called for a late-night consultation of doctors. When they equivocated, he sent for an old friend who told him bluntly, "You're done for."

Auguste died of pancreatic cancer two days later.

His funeral would have pleased him. After lying in state in an ebony and silver coffin, he was given an official funeral. The Invalides cannon boomed out hourly, and the cortege of soldiers, diplomats, clergy, and friends was over a mile long. His official carriage—symbolically empty—moved along slowly, draped in black. For service to the state, he was given 430 square feet at Père Lachaise and a mausoleum fit for a king—or, at least, for an unacknowledged prince.

DIVISION 55

This division is dominated by the huge monument of **Adolphe Thiers** (1797–1877). Although much of his work in France could be considered beneficial—leading the liberal party, attacking Napoléon III's imperialist policies and promoting Delacroix—it is overshadowed by his part in repressing the Commune (the revolt of Parisians against their own government's surrender to Germany in 1871 and plans to hand over the city without a fight). It was on Thiers' orders that army troops tracked the last of the Communards into the cemetery and shot every man, woman and child in cold blood. The Mur des Fédérés (Wall of the Federalists) in section 76 was erected in their memory.

One hundred years later Thiers' massive mausoleum is still a target for anti-fascist slogans. In 1985 it was sandblasted and cleaned to rid it of the guilty traces one more time.

DIVISION 56

By contrast, here lies an artist whose sympathies were always on the side of the people:

LOUIS DAVID *b. August 30. 1748, Paris; d. December 29, 1825, Brussels.* Looking at the inscription on David's tomb that reads, "His heart is in this grave near the body of his wife, companion in his misfortunes," one gets the impression of a sorrowful life—particularly if one also remembers that he was nicknamed the Artist of the Guillotine.

Yet David was no wilted flower, beaten down by the storms of French history. He chose his own destiny, selecting his issues, and was too stubborn to back down when challenged. His paintings, with their clear bright colors and exact delineation, are the work of a man who had no patience with fuzzy edges—in life or in art.

Even so, he edged gradually into the life of a revolutionary. Studying in Italy under a Prix de Rome from the Academy, he was attracted to classical themes and the Graeco-Roman ideal of beauty. His initial paintings had names like *Apollo and Diana Piercing the Children of Niobe with Arrows* and *Oath of the Horatii.* Returning to Paris, he continued in a historical vein with libertarian overtones, until he became aware of the Revolution fomenting around him. Realizing that he was in agreement with many of its aims, David organized patriotic celebrations, called for the execution of Louis XVI, and pledged to drink the cup of hemlock with Robespierre. He recorded the deaths of all the revolutionary martyrs from Marat to Joseph Barra, and sketched Marie Antoinette on her way to the guillotine. His enthusiasm ran rampant until, during one of the constant witch hunts among the party, he lost favor and was imprisoned.

The case against him was thin. He was in prison for about six months and during that time was allowed to paint, even requesting models. Although he was sobered by his incarceration, his patriotic ardor was soon rekindled with the coming of Napoléon. Given the title First Painter to the Emperor, he did several portraits of Napoléon, including an idealized one on horseback and another in his classic hand-inside-jacket pose.

Again, David's involvement in politics nearly destroyed him. He sided loyally with Napoléon during the Emperor's brief encore in 1815 and, after Waterloo, was branded an "irreconcilable enemy of France" and ordered to leave the country within 30 days. It was hinted that he could be exempted from this decree, but the artist refused special treatment. He and his wife packed and headed for Brussels.

Mme David was indeed loyal. At the height of the Revolution David had divorced her for "political reasons" (whatever those might have been), but once he was imprisoned they were quickly reconciled. She bore him at least four children and with evident good humor; her portrait by him shows a potato-nosed woman with coarse country features but a very engaging expression. His portraits were actually the best part of his work, though he did not value them as highly as his allegories.

Oddly enough, the King negotiated to buy several of the exiled artist's paintings. But when David died at 77 the government refused to let his body be brought home for burial. It was no more than political pique; before he died, David could have petitioned France for a recall, but he was too proud—and too scornful of the Bourbons—to do so. The Bourbons refused to let death do the asking for him.

Also in this section is the grave of **Raymond Radiguet** (1903–1923), a small and quiet monument in contrast with the flamboyance of his short life. One of Cocteau's amours, he allegedly shaved his head with an oyster shell, wore a monocle, and carried a cane—giving him the appearance of the precocious infant in New Year's Eve illustrations. Raymond wrote two volumes of poetry and a novel, *Le Diable au Corps* (The Devil in the Flesh, 1923) before he died at 20 of typhoid fever—misdiagnosed as the flu and treated with injections of salt water.

DIVISION 60

Valentin Haüy (1745–1822). Although not so well known as Braille, Haüy was a hero in his own right. As a young man he witnessed a mock orchestra of blind men in a café wearing huge cardboard spectacles and donkey ears, and trying to play instruments without strings. Their leader hit the musicians regularly, to the applause of the crowd. Haüy resolved to work for reform. He established a school for the blind—who were thought to be mentally retarded— and developed a system of raised roman letters. Louis Braille attended the school that Haüy founded.

DIVISION 66

This section's most important resident is impressionist painter Georges Seurat, whose only recognition here is his name inscribed on the inner wall of the small family mausoleum.

GEORGES SEURAT *b. December 2, 1859, Paris; d. March 29, 1891, Paris.* The real life of Georges Seurat is even more poignant than that portrayed in Stephen Sondheim's play,

Sunday in the Park with George. The child of a middle-class mother and an eccentric father who collected religious lithographs and lived by himself most of the time, Georges' tomb continues the secretiveness with which he carefully shrouded himself during his life.

As a young man, Georges discovered that he was good at art and began to study at the Ecole des Beaux-Arts. His approach was always intellectual, based on complex theories of color and perception, never simply a matter of looking at a subject, then daubing dots on a canvas—though some of his followers were less scrupulous than he in following the theory of Pointillism. Indeed, Georges himself commented that, "The more there are of us, the less original we will be, and on the day when everybody is using the technique, it will become worthless."

Georges was always willing to climb down from his studio ladder and discuss his techniques with visitors, but his personal life was a closed book. It was only after his death that his closest friends discovered he had had a mistress and child. Madeleine Knoblock appears in his painting *Young Woman Powdering Herself* as an extremely buxom, double-chinned femme with red hair piled high and in bangs.

Preparing for an outdoor exhibit, Seurat developed a throat infection and died at 31. Unlike Sondheim's hint of an American descendent, Georges' only child, a 13-month-old son, died a few days later of the same ailment. Madeleine disappeared from sight, perhaps returning to her native Alsace. The paintings which Georges left her are now in museums.

Outside of his largest and most famous work, *Sunday on La Grande Jatte*, and three other substantial canvases, Seurat's life's work seems small, totaling only about two hundred paintings and seven hundred drawings. Yet his Grand Jatte figures are as familiar to casual viewers as Van Gogh's *Sunflowers* or Toulouse-Lautrec's *Moulin Rouge*. And, as Sondheim's sensitive play points out, Georges would not let anything distract him from his own vision.

DIVISION 67

In this section the emphasis is on two mausoleums, one of them exhibiting a hand under glass.

The first is that of the chocolate-producing family of **Emile Justin Menier** (1826–1881) with friezes of cupids around wreaths which encircle the letter *M*.

The other belongs to the **Comte d'Ornano**, better known as the husband of **Marie Walewska**. Marie, a high-spirited young woman, gave birth to Napoléon's first son, Alexandre, in 1810 after meeting the Emperor when he visited Warsaw. (The Polish provisional government hinted that to indulge Napoléon's craving would help Poland politically.) Although she remained loyal to Napoléon, begging to be allowed to come and live with him on St. Helena, he persuaded her to stay with Walewski, 49 years her senior, whom she had married to save her family from financial ruin.

No doubt it is her hand under glass, but why it is there remains a secret.

DIVISION 68

Two composers inhabit this section. One is **Georges Enesco** (1881–1955) the most important Romanian composer who did much to establish a Romanian school of national music. Enesco's music combines many Romanian folk elements with a more cosmopolitan style which grew out of his education and residence in Paris. His most popular pieces remain his *Romanian Rhapsodies*, although his Third Piano Sonata, Third Orchestral Suite, and his neglected opera, *Oedipe*, are better indications of his talent. A virtuoso violinist, his students included Ferras, Grimiaux, and Menuhin. He was also the godfather of another Romanian, Dinu Lipatti, one of this century's great pianists. The composer lies in a plain cement tomb with his name in bas relief.

The other composer is best known for his fiery death scenes in *Carmen*.

GEORGES BIZET b. *October 25, 1838, Paris; d. June 3, 1875, Paris.* The bust of Bizet, which tops his tomb like a doll's head on a fence post, looks prophetically heavenward. It is the gaze of a man begging to be removed from a situation he finds distasteful—a request which was granted to him all too soon. The young Bizet, who resembled Paul McCartney wearing John Lennon's glasses, was high-spirited and quick-tempered. He was also given to self-doubt. The success which always just eluded him led to depression and contributed to his death.

Bizet was musically precocious, a gift carefully nurtured by talented parents. Entering the Conservatoire at nine, he won all the prizes, culminating in the Prix de Rome in 1857—a stipend which allowed him three years' study in Italy. He had narrowed his field of interest to light opera, and his future stretched ahead of him like a Gilbert and Sullivan sea.

Unfortunately a composer cannot write light opera by

himself, and Bizet searched endlessly for suitable librettos. As a student he had been assigned several old war-horses more deserving of burial than enhancement. He did little better finding stories on his own. Some of his finest music is in *The Pearl-Fishers*, but the opera is spoiled by a weak text.

While writing operettas that were panned, Bizet married his sweetheart Geneviève Halévy and had a son, Jacques. Domestic life calmed his eagerness to pick fights, and he grew plump on the chocolates and petits fours his students fed him. He was a loving father to Jacques and also to Jean Reiter, the son of his parents' former maid, who, as was much later revealed, was his son as well. The only serious distraction from his music was his wife. Geneviève Bizet was high-strung and kept him busy looking after her emotional difficulties.

When Bizet finally found a good story in *Carmen*, he almost failed to get it staged because of its subject matter. One of the lyricists, his father-in-law Ludovic Halévy, had to assure the opera's skeptical director that the thieves were "comic gypsies" and that Carmen would be "softened, toned down." Even so, director de Leuven begged him, "Please try not to have her die. Death on the stage of the Opéra-Comique! Such a thing has never been seen!"

Yet Carmen did die in the end, preferring to be stabbed rather than be untrue to herself. The singer who played her, Galli-Marié, was wonderfully dramatic. Perhaps too dramatic, for the critics' antipathy was intensified at the work's having a "lawless, heartless prostitute" as a heroine. In their self-righteousness they overlooked the opera's music and its timeless themes.

Bizet died depressed by yet another failure, succumbing at 36 to a combination of maladies: throat abscesses, rheumatic fever, a tumor inside his ear, and a heart attack. He was also worn down by a marriage which demanded too much emotional energy and exhausted by his failure to live up to his early promise.

Wealthy from the royalties earned by *Carmen*, his widow was courted by Guy de Maupassant among many others and eventually married Emile Straus, a lawyer with Rothschild connections. Geneviève Halévy Bizet Straus established a brilliant salon and was immortalized by Marcel Proust as the duchess in *The Guermantes Way*. Sadly, Bizet missed both the blossoming of his wife and the blossoming of his opera. Standing by his monument, one wishes he could at least know how his *Carmen* has captivated the world.

DIVISION 71

One of the most talked-about monuments in the ceme-
tery, that of **Crocé-Spinelli** and **Sivel** (no other identification is given on the tomb), is located here on the corner of
Avenue Circulaire. These two balloonists ascended twenty-
six thousand feet over India and were asphyxiated when
the air grew too thin. Their monument displays them presumably naked but covered from the chest down, side-by-
side, hand-in-hand, in tribute to their comradeship in life
and death.

DIVISION 74 (Père Lachaise: Tour One)

Rosa Bonheur (1822–1899) in a simple tomb decorated
with palm fronds. A painter of animal life, her most famous

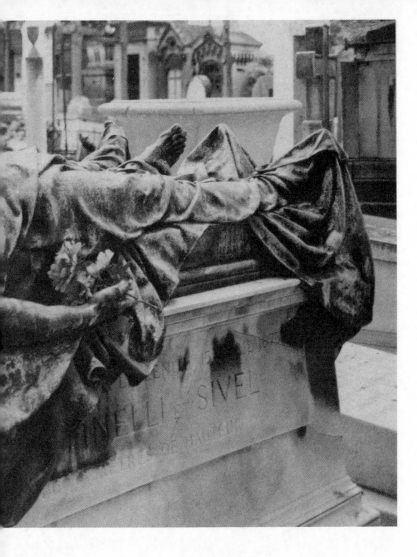

work, *The Horse Fair*, is in New York's Metropolitan Museum of Art.

DIVISION 76 (Père Lachaise: Tour Four)

In this narrow section are two graves of interest. One is that of **Laura Marx** (1846–1911) and **Paul Lafargue** (1842–1911), Karl Marx's daughter and son-in-law who, for reasons unknown to us, committed suicide together in 1911 by injections of cyanide. The very simple tomb also holds their grandson, **Karl-Jean Marx** (1904–1981), a sculptor.

On the outside closest to the street is the Mur des Fédérés. A plaque marks the place where members of the Commune were tracked down and shot here on May 24, 1871.

C H A P T E R 4

PÈRE LACHAISE
Tour Four

▲ ▲ ▲

DIVISION 81

TWO ACTRESSES SHARE this section. **Virginie Déjazet** (1797–1875) packed them in for years before being laid to rest in this family monument. **Julie Feygine** (1861–1882), a tempestuous redhead, was a suicide at 2l for unrequited love of the Duc de Morny.

DIVISION 85

An extremely discreet mausoleum with no name outside is all that marks the remains of General **Rafael Molina Trujillo** (1891–1961), dictator of St. Dominique, who was tracked down and assassinated by his enemies. Trujillo, who had lived by the machine gun, invited such responses. His enemies, not content with having shot him, beheaded him, keeping his head as well. Perhaps he is buried quietly in Paris, where he had family, to prevent further desecration.

Farther along is the family monument of:

MARCEL PROUST b. *July 10, 1871, Paris; d. November 18, 1922, Paris.* Devotees of *Remembrance of Things Past* will surely be disappointed by Proust's grave. As a writer who specialized in emotional minutia, exquisitely detailing the sunlight on a chest of drawers and cataloging the emotions that occur just before sleep, he deserves a monument as carved and complicated as a medieval cathedral.

But Marcel's grave is more his father's than his own. The bronze visage on an otherwise plain expanse is that of Dr. Adrian Proust, one of the foremost doctors of his era, best

Opposite: Oranienbour and Sachsenhausen memorial

(A) Isadora Duncan
(B) Apollinaire
(C) Jean Pezon
(D) Julie Feygine
(E) Virginie Déjazet
(F) Marcel Proust
(G) Général Trujillo
(H) Harriet Toby
(I) Marie Laurencin
(J) Delage family
(K) Oscar Wilde
(L) Bain family
(M) Daumy family

(N) Gertrude Stein
    Alice B. Toklas
(P) Paul Eluard
(R) Edith Piaf
(S) Edouard Drumont
(T) Théophile Gramme
(U) Maroun-Khadra
(V) Victor Noir
(W) Paul Doucherat
(X) victims of the
    Comic Opera fire
(Y) Amodeo Modigliani

known for his successful crusade to keep cholera out of France. Marcel's younger brother Robert, also buried here, was a gynecologist. Marcel had extensive medical knowledge, but he practiced only on himself. In a family of high achievers, his life seemed as meandering to his parents as his writings did to his critics.

Dr. Proust never withheld money for the exquisite clothes Marcel favored, the long cab rides, orchids and roses, intimate dinners for 12 or 15, and enough medications to stock a pharmacy, but he did pay the bills with a sigh. The expense list hints at both Marcel's complicated relationships and his hypochondria.

There are indications that he enjoyed ill health because he thought his mother loved him more when he was sick; indeed, at times his life appeared to be one long quest for her undivided attention. But this was never to be. Jeanne Proust, happily married and accustomed to putting her husband above everyone else, followed Adrian into the family plot in 1905, two years after his death at 56. Dying of nephritis, she was still able to play a favorite family game, that of applying classical quotations to immediate situations. When the hospital nurse finally left the room, she quipped to Marcel, "I never saw a better-timed departure" (Molière) and exhorted her son, "If you're no Roman, then deserve to be one!" (Horace).

Marcel was devastated by her death, though he lingered on for 17 years before succumbing to pneumonia. By then he had completed his epic 16-volume work, which his

PÈRE LACHAISE: Tour Four

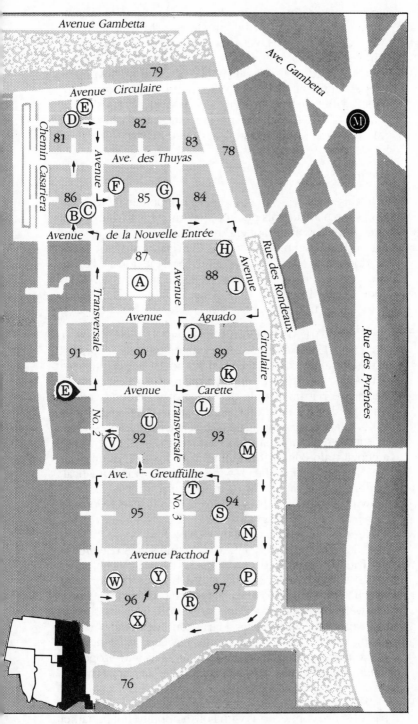

parents never knew about. It remains a stunning accomplishment, a portrait of his life and world which sweeps over several decades, yet moves in attentively to capture minute flutters of emotion.

Proust died at 44 Rue Hamelin, attended by his housekeeper and brother Robert. With him died the special intensity with which he scrutinized the world and translated it into words. A friend, seeing him laid out, commented, "Marcel looks deader than other dead people." Everyone knew what he meant.

DIVISION 86

In this section is the monument of lion tamer, **Jean Pezon**, shown astride his pet lion, Brutus, who ate him—one does not know if it happened in a moment of pique or if Brutus had been plotting to end the relationship for years. No doubt they are buried together, for if the lion ate Pezon, and Pezon is here. . . . In any case, the happy couple has been lionized here.

In this section is also the tomb of the still-beloved poet:

GUILLAUME APOLLINAIRE *b. August 31, 1880, Rome; d. Nov. 9, 1918, Paris.* The tall and dignified stele, engraved with several stanzas of Apollinaire's poetry and a calligram with *Mon coeur pareil a une flamme renversée* (My heart is like an everlasting fire) in the shape of a valentine, calls to mind a slender neurasthenic romantic. The anonymous roses left regularly on his grave add to that impression.

But the real Apollinaire was attractive more in the way of a genial train conductor. Plump from his love of fine cuisine, his pear-shaped head (wider at the chin) and practically nonexistent mouth were immortalized many times in drawings by his good friend Picasso: Apollinaire as Pope, as clown, as soldier, as gymnast.

He and his wife **Jacqueline Kolb**, who is also buried here, had been married only a few months when he died at 38; friends speculated that if he had lived much longer there would have been gun shots. But the relationships which inspired his most yearning love poetry came earlier and were either stormy or unconsummated. The most notable were with fellow artist Marie Laurencin and a chaste young English governness, Annie Playden. At 21 he took Annie to a romantic spot in the mountains and proposed. When she declined his "fortune and title," he threatened to throw her down a precipice.

As far as a title went, his mother, Olga de Kostrowitzky, had obscure connections with Polish nobility, but his father was unknown even to Guillaume. His fortune was imaginary. Olga's profession was of the sort that got them quickly banished from middle-class neighborhoods, and Guillaume and his younger brother Albert were once implicated in a scheme to slip out of a Belgian hotel owing many months rent.

Apollinaire first published poetry in little magazines and then went on to write art criticism and *Les Peintres Cubistes* (The Cubist Painters, 1913) but his real fame came from two poetry collections, *Alcools* (Alcohol, 1913) and *Calligrammes* (Calligrams, 1918). As a very young man he had a fondness for scatalogical language and wrote pornography as a sideline.

Apollinaire changed his destiny by enlisting in World War I. He acquitted himself well until a head wound in 1916 necessitated first an operation to remove splinters of shell and, eventually, a trepanning (skull perforation to remove pressure). His health was affected adversely. He returned to Paris, met and married Jacqueline, and was adopted by the surrealists. But he then succumbed to influenza.

He did not go without protest. He begged the doctor, "Save me! I still have so many things to say!" Most of his family followed him within a few months. His mother and her long-term paramour, Jules Weil, also died in the flu epidemic, and his brother Alfred perished in Mexico. The only one left untouched was Jacqueline. Rather unromantically, she lived on for another 50 years.

DIVISION 87

The Columbarium (crematorium), which is still used, dominates this division. Instead of tombs there are compartments for ashes, many of them individualized. Here reside French composer **Paul Dukas** (1865–1935) of *The Sorcerer's Apprentice* fame; American **Loie Fuller** (1862–1928), who performed her interpretive dancing with scarves and is well-represented on art deco lamps; and, in compartment 6796, an even more famous American dancer:

ISADORA DUNCAN *b. May 27, 1878, San Francisco; d. September 14, 1927, Nice.* Everyone who saw the movie *Isadora* remembers the final scene: one moment Isadora is laughing gaily, climbing into a low-slung convertible. In the next, her head is yanked back, blue eyes sightless; the camera pans to her flowing scarf caught in the spokes of the wheel.

A grotesque death can sometimes trivialize the memory of a life, but the world mourned Isadora with the dignity she deserved. It had been 14 years since the death by drowning of her two beloved children, Deirdre and Patrick—also a freak accident, in which the limousine in which they were riding with their nurse rolled backward into the Seine. Then, too, the people of the world had united in their sympathy.

Her ordinary moments, however, inspired less reverence. Isadora was not a believer in marriage and felt that a woman was entitled to choose the best father for her children. Her first choice was Gordon Craig, the highly regard-

ed stage designer. The second was sewing machine heir, Paris Singer. After the drowning death of their children, Isadora had a third child by a young Italian sculptor who approached her on the beach when she was in mourning. Unfortunately, the baby lived only a few hours.

The Columbarium

In America her involvement with the Russian Revolution was always a subject of controversy. She was strongly in favor of the Bolsheviks and composed several dances to their revolutionary songs. She also married poet Sergei Yesenin. Sergei, 15 years younger than Isadora, had already been married at least twice (he was then 26) and had several children. Yet despite the language barrier and Sergei's proclivity for drunken scenes, they lived together several years before Sergei left her in 1924, intending to marry again. (He never did; in 1925 he hanged himself.)

Isadora was committed to the highest ideals of truth and beauty, which she expressed through interpretive dancing: a combination of mime and graceful motions set to classical music. Strongly influenced by Greek mythology and philosophy, she danced in flowing Hellenic garments, and at one point she and her family—mother, sister Elizabeth, brothers Augustin and Raymond—visited Greece and bought land to build a temple to aesthetic ideals. (The project was abandoned when no water supply was found.)

Isadora scorned classical ballet as too mannered and sterile and created a choreography all her own. During her adulthood she ran schools at various times to teach her philosophy of dance. A number of the little girls grew up to be performers—if not the super race she intended—but Isadora tended to forget the children and go off on adventures of her own. The legacy she left to modern dance was her innovative exploration of the depths of a piece of great music and her expressive interpretation of it. She is not remembered for specific techniques.

Isadora's life ebbed and flowed rather than ascended to any pinnacle, but toward the end of it she seemed worn out. Perhaps when she died at 48, her ashes mingling with her children's in the Columbarium, death did not seem wholly unwelcome.

Among the most interesting monuments here are numbers 6915 and 6925. These adjacent compartments each have a hand reaching out toward the other, the fingertips just touching.

DIVISION 88

The plain granite tomb of **Marie Laurencin** (1885–1956) scarcely gives a clue to her eccentric and colorful personality. Fey and charming, she drifted through the Paris twenties scene with a blank expression because of her extreme nearsightedness; her art was airy and primitive with soft, flat colors. Later on she became a successful textile and wallpaper designer and did the sets for Diaghilev's production of Poulenc's *Les Biches* (The Deer).

Rather fittingly, Marie lies near Apollinaire, her tempestuous lover for six years, and Gertrude Stein, to whom she made her first sale of a painting.

Also in this section, and one of the first monuments you see on entering from Avenue du Père Lachaise, is that of **Harriet Toby** (1929–1952). The ballet dancer on the tomb, caught in an eternal pirouette, represents Miss Toby, who died at 22 in an airplane crash in Nice.

DIVISION 89

Famille Delage, whose monument—a substantial, truncated pyramid—is topped by a large green pelican, an early Christian symbol.

And finally, as unique and striking in death as in life:

OSCAR WILDE *b. October 16, 1854, Dublin; d. November 30, 1900, Paris.* In death as in life, Oscar Wilde's privates were a cause for public concern. Wilde, an Irishman who authored *The Picture of Dorian Gray, The Importance of Being Earnest*, and *Salomé*, spent two years in prison after being convicted of homosexual acts and died three years after his release, broken by the harsh jail conditions.

After a wait of nine years in Bagneaux Cemetery, Wilde's

Jacob Epstein's monument to Oscar Wilde

remains were transferred to Père Lachaise on July 19, 1909. (The doctors had advised that he be buried in quicklime to reduce the body to bone before transfer. Instead, the substance preserved him, shocking the gravediggers; his hair and beard had even grown longer.)

It took Jacob Epstein three years to sculpt his monument, which represents the poet as a winged messenger, done in an Egyptian art deco style. When Epstein arrived to put the finishing touches on the statue, he found it shrouded and guarded by a gendarme; the cemetery conservateur had found it "indecent" and had it banned.

Officials refused to bow to public intellectual pressure until an acceptable alteration was made—a plaque serving as a fig leaf. The tomb was unveiled in 1914, but by 1922 students, in nocturnal raids, had hacked away the fig leaf as well as a substantial portion of what lay beneath. (A richer story is that two Englishwomen, offended at Wilde's being publicly portrayed as so well-endowed, committed the emasculation themselves. The conservateur, after finding the parts at the monument's base, is supposed to have used them as paperweights.)

Wilde was considered by many of his illustrious contemporaries to be the greatest conversationalist of his time, outranking such masters as Swinburne, George Meredith, and Henry James. His epigrams still retain their wit and acuity, but in retrospect his works seem to lack substance. Wilde said himself that the great drama of his life was "that I've put my genius into my life; I've only put my talent into my works."

After his release from jail, he talked about involving himself in prison reforms (especially for children) but could not muster up the effort. He completed only *The Ballad of Reading Gaol*, from which come the prophetic words on the back of his tomb:

> And alien tears will fill for him
> Pity's long broken urn
> For his mourners will be outcast men
> And outcasts always mourn.

DIVISION 91

Auguste Blanqui (1805–1881), socialist and professional revolutionary, best known as president of the short-lived Paris Commune. Between 1831 and 1879 he spent 33 years in prison for his political views.

DIVISION 92

This section holds several intriguing tombs.

At the back of the section, along Avenue Transversale No. 1, is the monument of **Victor Noir** (1848–1870), a journalist who criticized Pierre Bonaparte, Napoléon III's cousin, and was shot to death by him in return. His monument is a notable work of funerary, showing Noir life-sized even to top hat, and is thought to have special powers. Young wives, wishing to get pregnant, have traditionally rubbed a certain

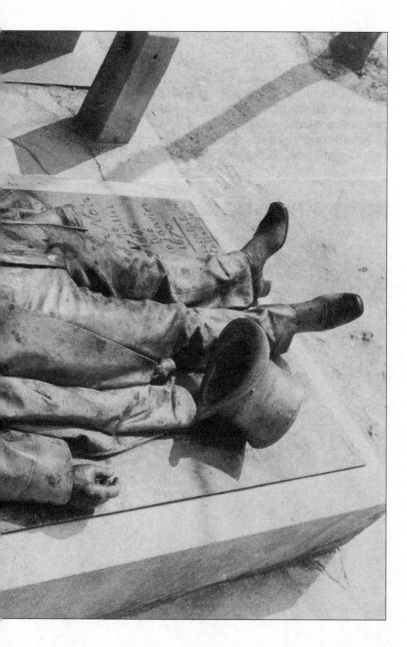

portion of his anatomy for luck. Judging from the brightness of the area, one might conclude that this, like most myths, has some validity. The hat serves as a receptacle for prayers and love notes.

Toward the center of this section is a tomb that, because of its bright white stone and subject matter, is set apart from all others. It belongs to **Maroun-Khadra**, about whom little is known, and tenderly depicts a mother lying in bed nursing her newborn child. Set among the sepulchral greys and blacks of surrounding slabs, crosses, headstones, and mausoleums, the effect of the carving is all the more powerful and touching; this intimate moment of life and birth, of love and nourishment, of the cycle of life, speaks far more poignantly and eloquently than the many pompous offerings to ego found throughout the cemetery.

Maroun-Khadra

DIVISION 93

In this division is a group of interesting graves belonging to otherwise anonymous souls.

Along the Avenue Circulaire is the monument of the **Daumy** family, which shows a woman in 1920's dress set in a framework of Greek pillars. Her hand lightly caresses the head and ear of her dog. Next to her, in an even more classical setting, is a lonely young woman seated on a stone bench within a semicircle of formal columns, wistfully staring into the distance.

On the Avenue Carette, in white stone, is a carving of a seminude woman draped across the top of the stone, with her head reclining on a broken column. Finally, farther along is the tomb of the **Bain** family, which has the look of a florid, tiered cake decorated with children, a dog, papa, and topped with an ornate cross.

DIVISION 94

Théophile Gramme (1826–1901), Belgian engineer who in 1869 invented the first continuous current electrical generator, giving rise to the development of electric power. He is shown sitting in a chair, holding his invention—the Gramme dynamo—on his lap.

The tomb of a French magistrate, **Roger**, is dramatically marked by a cowled figure standing under a pointed arch, robed hands held to his face. Save for the tip of a shoe, there is nothing human visible in this stylised sculpting. It nevertheless exudes a powerful sense of grief coupled with a sense of monastic stoicism.

Edouard Drumont (1844–1917), a gifted writer who unfortunately used his talents to promote anti-Semitism through his paper *La Libre Parole* and his book *La France Juive* (Jewish France, 1886). The writings not only formed a basis and rallying point for the growing mood of anti-Semitism in France, but they also directly challenged the wisdom of having too many Jews in important army positions. The articles gathered support, and with support came more blatant prejudice, eventually providing the background and footing for the Dreyfus Affair.

And finally, in a grave that is certain to disappoint any of their admirers, Gertrude Stein and Alice B. Toklas. The plot appears forgotten, for not only is it bereft of flowers, but it is overgrown with weeds. Those put off by Stein's arrogance might find some justice in this, but certainly so influential a person deserves a better remembrance. The relationship remains intact: Gertrude featured on the front of the headstone, Alice listed quietly on the back.

GERTRUDE STEIN *b. February 3, 1874, Allegheny, Penn-sylvania; d. July 27, 1946, Paris.* **ALICE B. TOKLAS** *b. April 30 1877, San Francisco; d. March 7, 1967, Paris.* Gertrude Stein was given her personality at birth. Egocentric, powerful, and intellectually self-confident, she wavered only in her choice of a career. Stein studied philosophy at Radcliffe and completed everything but an obstetrics exam at Johns Hop-kins Medical School before traveling to Paris to visit her brother Leo and discovering her true vocation, literature. She had also found her spiritual home and never consid-ered living anywhere else.

Most people remember Gertrude Stein for the salon she kept, which included Hemingway, Fitzgerald, Sherwood Anderson, Matisse, Picasso, and Virgil Thomson. But Ger-trude saw herself primarily as a writer, presenting literature as a cubist portrait by viewing the subject again and again without plot progression, and divesting language of its liter-al meanings. She had to subsidy-publish *Three Lives* in 1910, but in 1914 a small avant-garde firm, Claire Marie, brought out *Tender Buttons* with the blurb, "She is a ship that flies no flag and she is outside the law of art, but she descends on every port and leaves a memory of her visit."

Alice B. Toklas came to Paris from San Francisco in 1906. She was a darkly intense young woman with a faint mous-tache, whose schooling had been in the arts of cooking, needlework and literature. It appears to have been love at first sight. After Alice moved in, Leo—from whom Gertrude had become increasingly estranged—soon moved out. Al-ice cooked, typed Gertrude's manuscripts, and eventually handled all the details to make their lives run smoothly. She outlived Gertrude by nearly 20 years and during that time produced three books, most notably *The Alice B. Toklas Cookbook.*

Would Gertrude Stein, who was immortalized in so many paintings and sculptures, have been satisfied with such a plain slab, fronted by a now-abandoned bed of earth? She herself might have chosen Jo Davidson's unfor-gettable sculpture of her sitting crosslegged as a massive, brooding Buddha. Certainly she would have spelled Alle-gheny correctly and gotten her date of death right.

Yet even in the throes of death she was more concerned with what things meant than how they looked. Her last words to Alice were, "What is the answer?" And when her longtime companion was silent, she added, "Well, then, what is the question?"

DIVISION 95

André Gill (Gosset de Guines, 1840–1885), the most famous caricaturist of his time, specialized in drawing oversized heads with tiny bodies.

DIVISION 96

Here lie the unidentified victims of the fire at the Comic Opera in 1887, and, in an extremely simple grave, victims of another kind:

AMODEO MODIGLIANI *b. July 12, 1884, Livorno, Italy; d. January 24, 1920, Paris.* **JEANNE HERBUTERNE** *b. April 6, 1898, Paris; d. January 25, 1920, Paris.* The life of Modigliani is reminiscient of a drawing in which a person enters a revolving door and comes out looking entirely different. A strikingly handsome young man, given to easy conquests, "Modi" came to Paris from Leghorn, Italy, in 1906. He was nattily dressed, carrying with him a purse full of money and firm ideas of how an artist should look (dapper), live (graciously), and paint (conventionally).

When he staggered out of Paris 14 years later (and into Père Lachaise) he had been ravaged by the effects of alcohol, opium, and the strain of struggling to interest people in his art. He was also plagued by tuberculosis and given to black moods; only his painting had improved.

Modigliani's style, with its flat colors and peaceful elongated faces, still baffles many people. It takes a discerning eye to recognize the individuality of each portrait. Yet portraits were all that interested him. He regarded landscapes as backgrounds at best and shouted down opponents with, "Don't make me laugh. Landscapes simply do not exist!"

What did exist for Modi were living people: his mother back in Italy, his friends Soutine, Utrillo, and art dealer Zborowski, various lovers, and, eventually, Jeanne Hebuterne and his baby daughter, Jeanne.

Jeanne Hebuterne, the other occupant of this grave, was about 17 when she first met Modigliani. She was an art student and the child of conservative Catholic parents who attempted to disown her for her liason with a depraved and unsuccessful Jewish painter. Jeanne, who spoke very rarely, turned her back on them and adored her "husband." He reciprocated by painting 20 portraits of her, although baby Jeanne was the true apple of his eye.

Jeanne Hebuterne was artistically talented but emotionally weak. She could not care for their baby, who was boarded in the country in a foster care arrangement. When Amodeo was dying she did not even try to get a doctor, knowing his dislike for them and fearing his displeasure. At the time, Jean was also heavily pregnant with their second child.

The situation ended on January 22, 1920, when, after a week of being unable to move, Modigliani was taken to Hospital de la Charité. He died two days later of tubercular meningitis. Jeanne has been variously described as calm, depressed, dazed, and insane with grief at that point. She went to stay at her parents' apartment and, on the dawn of January 25th, threw herself from a fifth-story window.

Her parents reacted badly. They refused to bring her body inside (the workman who found her had to bring her back to the old, rat-infested studio). Then they buried her as secretly as they could in far-off Bagneux Cemetery— despite the pleadings of Jeanne's and Modigliani's friends.

In 1930 the Hebuternes relented and allowed her remains to be placed with her lover's in Père Lachaise. Perhaps the passing of time had tempered their grief, and Modigliani's increased reputation as an artist had lent respectability to the tragedy. And perhaps they had come to terms with the realization that this was what their daughter would have wanted.

Finally, along Avenue Transversal No. 2, is a man being victimized on his own tomb. **Paul Doucherot** (1869–1943) is shown as Prometheus bound to the rock, with the vulture dipping deep into his side.

DIVISION 97

All along the perimeter of this division on the Avenue Circulaire are memorials to the victims of the concentration camps. Walking from Avenue Pachtod toward the corner, the first one you will see is the memorial to the six hundred thousand French deportees (concentration camp prisoners) who were forced to labor for the Germans. The monument also honors the sixty thousand who died, the fifteen thousand resistance fighters who were shot, hanged, or decapitated, and the fifty thousand persons missing and never accounted for. The sculpting shows a worker chained to a wheel which is crushing another fettered inmate.

Immediately adjacent is the memorial to the victims of **Oranienburg** and **Sachsenhausen**. The large, emaciated figure is dramatically held aloft amid flames. Next is the monument displaying three skeletal inmates of **Buchenwald-Dora**. One of them has lost his will to live; the other two are attempting to keep him from sinking into death.

On the sloping curve we find an abstract figure outlined only with vague, anonymous features. It is the **Auschwitz** memorial. Many small individual markers have been placed on its large stone base which contains a commemorative script. In the same area, rising up behind a hedge, are the despairing fettered hands of the **Ravensbruck** monument.

The **Neuengamme** monument poignantly shows a woman grasping a block of stone; her expression is unreadable, self-contained. On the corner the **Mauthausen** monument depicts the 186 steps up which the inmates of this concentration camp were forced to carry rocks from its quarry. The oppressive loads of this forced labor took a heavy toll on the spirits as well as the lives of the inmates.

Also buried in this section is **Paul Eluard** (Eugène Grindel, 1895–1952), a founder of surrealism, who moved from experimental to political poetry when he joined the Communist party.

Edith Piaf is buried in a simple black tomb much like the little black dress she wore when she was performing.

EDITH GIOVANNA GASSION (PIAF) *b. December 19, 1915, Paris; d. October 10, 1963, Plascassier.* Edith Gassion; *la môme Piaf* (the little sparrow); Edith Piaf. Her successive names illustrate the merging of the person Gassion with the performer Piaf and her growth into one of the great performers of the century. Childlike in size and behavior, she never outgrew the deprivation of a childhood marked by neglect and periodic abandonment by her parents, of being raised for six years in a brothel, of earning a squalid independence at 15 as a street singer, and, at 19, losing her 2-year-old daughter, Marcelle, to menningitis.

In hopes of stilling these memories, she lived a passionate life at a furious pace. She was only partially successful; she might for a while forget, but she never outgrew the childish qualities which contributed to both her greatness and her downfall.

Piaf craved and depended on love and attention. Her lovers were legion; she rarely spent a night without a man by her side. She frequently fell in love, certain that each new man was her one true love, only to soon become disenchanted. Oftentimes she would cheat on her lovers, and none too subtly, hoping to keep the emotions of all alive. She was impulsive and demanded immediate gratification. Favorite movies would be seen ad nauseum, and no excuse was needed to party; indeed, most nights called for long hours of dining and drinking with friends. When she had the money, she paid the tab. It was through such extravagance that even her famous one thousand dollar-per-night fees would disappear.

Yet she was generous and devoted. She aided the resistance in World War II. And she gave her time and attention to up-and-coming performers including Yves Montand and Charles Aznavour. What she demanded in return was loyalty and devotion.

As if to make up for the chaos of her life, Piaf demanded from herself an extraordinary degree of discipline and dedication in her art. She worked through, in her singing, not only the sorrows of her childhood but those of her adult life as well—the deaths by plane crash of her self-proclaimed greatest love, boxer Marcel Cerdan, and of a later love, Douglas Davies. There was the pain and disability brought on by three car crashes and rheumatism, her subsequent addiction to morphine, and her longer-standing dependence on alcohol. Despite these afflictions, in later life she courageously persevered and, singing an increasing number of autobiographical songs, achieved her greatest triumphs on stage.

Piaf's talent and fame helped her to meet and form friendships with people such as Marlene Dietrich and Jean Cocteau. Yet her primary love and allegiance remained with the working class from which she came. At her funeral forty thousand people broke through the barricades at Père Lachaise to pay her homage.

In the end one central image remains: a small, frail-looking woman standing alone in the circle of a spotlight, her pale face and hands set off by a plain black dress, her feet slightly apart. Her arms are occasionally spread, but otherwise there is nothing to distract. Contrasting with this classical study in black and white is the color of the voice—clear, coarse, and strong, cutting through the hall to deliver all the passion and pathos of the song and the life, "Non, Je ne regrette rien."

C H A P T E R   5

THE PANTHÉON

▲   ▲   ▲

*Let us now praise famous men
and our fathers that begat us.
They were honored in their
generations and were the glory
of their times.*

—ECCLESIASTICUS

LOGICALLY, THE PANTHÉON should be the crowning
point of a cemetery tour. It has more famous dust per
square inch than any other place in Paris. Its dome can be
seen from all over the city; up close it is equally imposing.
Notwithstanding all that, you may find it disappointing.

The Panthéon is situated on the highest point of the Left
Bank and can be reached by taking the Métro to the stop
bearing its name. Originally the Church of Sainte Geneviève, leaders of the French Revolution who were attempting to abolish anything religious decreed that it would
instead be a burial place for the great. Although from time
to time it subsequently reverted to Church use, it is once
again a national monument.

The main portico has a frieze by David d'Angers which
represents France crowning her distinguished sons with
laurels. Her most distinguished sons are not in the above-
ground edifice under the dome, however, but downstairs
in the basement crypt. To reach it, you must follow the signs
down the steps and inside. It is here you may feel some
dismay: the crypt is austere, rather like a jail, its inhabitants
scattered in cells behind grillwork. Even so, for a complete
tour of notable graves, this site should not be missed.

As you descend the outside stairs and enter the door to
the crypt, you will pass a memorial that contains the heart of
Léon Gambetta (1838–1882), a lawyer and revolutionary
active in the Commune and in shaping governmental poli-

cy. The next monuments, in alcoves facing each other, are those of two men who disliked each other intensely and would not have appreciated spending eternity together. Though they never physically met, they devoted much energy to villifying each other in print.

Rousseau's tomb is decorated by a painted carving of an arm reaching out of a closed door and holding a torch. Its implication of passing along Truth would no doubt have appealed to him greatly.

JEAN JACQUES ROUSSEAU *b. June 28, 1712, Geneva; d. July 2, 1778, Ermenonville.* Jean Jacques Rousseau's early life reads like a Dickens novel. When he was 10 days old, his beautiful mother died. As Rousseau was growing up, his sentimental father would initiate extravagant weeping sessions over his dead wife, then stay up happily till dawn reading novels aloud to the child. His older brother left home in adolescence never to be heard of again. When Jean Jacques was 13 he was apprenticed to a brutish engraver until he finally ran away.

On the road, the drama continued. Rousseau met a benevolent curé who steered him to Mme de Warens, a lovely young convert. She, unknown to Rousseau, received a stipend for every soul she rescued from Calvinism. His alarmed father sent a decidedly Dickensian couple, the Sabrans, to retrieve him. But instead of returning Jean Jacques to Geneva, they cheerfully (and in Mme de Warens' pay) escorted him to a Catholic seminary in Italy. Rousseau dutifully converted, then left to see what the next chapter had in store.

The drama was slow in developing. He tried his hand at many things—music copier and theorist, lackey, tutor, land-office clerk, secretary. At 38 he finally achieved the recognition he had been seeking with his essay, *Discourse on the Moral Effects of the Arts and Sciences.* It propelled him into the finest salons of Paris and launched a career in political writing. Widespread popularity came in 1761 with *Julie ou la Nouvelle Héloïse,* an epistolary novel of a young woman's fall from virtue and her subsequent recovery. Rousseau's *Confessions* with their intensely personal descriptions of the author's idiosyncrasies, feelings, and feuds, are all that is read of the author today; although his brilliant opening line "Man is born free but everywhere he is still in chains," from *The Social Contract* is still quoted.

If Jean Jacques' early life left him with a flair for drama, it also helped to cripple him emotionally. His study *Emile* is a charming rendition of a child educated the "natural" way, but none of his own five children were so lucky. At the birth of each he forced his common-law wife, Thérése, to carry the baby to the foundling home without identification—making future reunions impossible. With his genius for rationalization, he affirmed he was doing it to save Thérése from a reputation as a "loose woman."

Jean Jacques constantly tested his friends, the way a child pushes his parents to see how much their love will forgive, by demanding that they satisfy his whims while asserting that he owed them nothing; when a few of his friends forgave him anyway, he dropped them as idiots. By the time Rousseau died, writhing on the borders of paranoia, he was sworn public enemies with Diderot, Voltaire, and Hume and imagined he had been slighted by scores of others.

Jean Jacques' literary reputation was also at a low ebb at that point, but after his death of cerebral congestion (brought on by arteriosclerosis of the kidneys), it sprang back. By 1789 he was being hailed by Robespierre as a revolutionary martyr, and that year he was reburied in the Panthéon. Readers began to enjoy his posthumous *Confessions*, which helped to foster a new age of candor in literature. On the question of his real worth as a philosopher, based on his often-contradictory writings, the jury is still out.

To Rousseau's left, Voltaire smiles benignly in a statue created by Jean-Antoine Houdon. His bier, topped by what appears to be a cannonball, is behind him. Although Voltaire died the same year as Rousseau, he was brought here the year before his rival—a fact which would have pleased him.

VOLTAIRE (François Marie Arouet) *b. November 21, 1694, Paris; d. May 30, 1778, Paris.* Even though they had two countries at their disposal, France and Switzerland weren't big enough for both Rousseau and Voltaire. They began their battle with the usual flattery, Rousseau sending the older philosopher an idea with the comment, "I have worked 15 years to make myself worthy of your glance," and Voltaire responding, "After reading your book [*Treatise on the Origin of Inequality*], one feels like crawling around on all fours." But once each was sure the other knew of his existence, the gloves came off.

They fought because Rousseau could not get along with anyone for long; because Voltaire was welcome in Jean Jacques' native Geneva when he himself had been turned out; and because Voltaire, a practical man of action ("It is better to save a guilty man than to condemn an innocent one"), could not bear the romantic sensibilities of his rival.

When *La Nouvelle Héloïse* appeared, Voltaire published scathing attacks against it, rather unfairly using four different pseudynyms.

Voltaire was not without crotchets of his own. After his mother died when he was seven, Voltaire grew bored with his father's respectable family and, as soon as he could, cast doubts on his paternity, changing his name from Arouet to Voltaire. He was trained as a lawyer but preferred writing scandalous verses. Even a term in jail for offending the Regent did not deter him.

Voltaire's countenance, widely caricatured, was unmistakable: alert eyes, meandering nose, black curly wig, thin lips compressed in a smirk. He was not considered handsome, but he did have two major liasons in his life, one with Mme Emilie du Châtelet, a brilliant and witty woman and Newtonian scholar who died at 43 in unplanned childbirth (neither her husband nor Voltaire was the father). The other was with his widowed niece, Mme Denis, a plump and mean-spirited soul who consoled him after Emilie's passing.

Voltaire's finest hours were spent at Ferney, a small town near the Swiss border, which enabled him to move quickly to either country in case of persecution ("Philosophers should always have two or three underground holes in case of dogs hunting them"). Here he played lord of the manor and provided work for the local populace by creating a watch factory, a pottery, and a modern farm on his estate. He entertained everyone from Boswell and Gibbon to Casanova on the basis of a reputation that had been established by historical works such as *The Age of Louis XIV* and philosophical writings which included *Treatise on Tolerance* and *The Ignorant Philosopher*.

An attack by Rousseau against his poem on the earthquake of Lisbon (which questions Divine Providence) inspired Voltaire to create his masterpiece, *Candide*. In this satire the student Candide comes to realize that his mentor's philosophy "In this best of all possible worlds everything is for the best" does not hold up in the face of the manmade wars and natural disasters which were darkening the Age of Enlightenment.

Unfortunately, the man who said so much so brilliantly had a dark end. His death from uremia was slow and painful, and Mme Denis, by then his heir, did nothing to save him. A "nurse" had been hired by authorities, not to treat him but to record any blasphemies he uttered in case the family should again ask for a religious burial (already denied).

Despite the attitude of the clergy, he was still loved by the masses. Crowds outside his Paris apartment clamoured for his appearance on his balcony, while Voltaire, already dead, was being autopsied, embalmed, and dressed as if he were still alive. Propped in his carriage, he was taken to the Abbey of Seillières where his nephew, Abbé Migot, and a gathering of priests gave him a Christian burial. Church leaders in Paris protested, but he was allowed to remain there until the Revolution. At that point the man who had written, "If a man has tyrants he must overthrow them" was proclaimed a hero and reburied in the Panthéon with a huge procession and honors.

Very little of him is actually here. His heart, a foot, two teeth, and his "unusually large brain" were all seized at various times as private relics. His bones are alleged to have been removed in 1814 by religious extremists. But as a relative said at his Panthéonization, "His spirit is everywhere."

To find the others, continue into the next section, the Hall of Names. To your right are plaques honoring the dead of various wars. To your left are several more sets of cells. The plain cement biers in each are identical in design, though their metal floral wreaths differ slightly. In the first room are several political figures, of whom the best-known is **Lazare Carnot** (1753–1823), a mathematician turned military strategist. Active in the Revolution, he served under Napoléon and was exiled when royalty was restored in 1814.

In the second alcove are two writers, Emile Zola and Victor Hugo.

EMILE ZOLA b. *April 2, 1840, Paris; d. September 9, 1902, Paris.* In the same way that the spirit of a loved one seems to linger nearby right after death, the effects of Emile Zola's life continued after his life ceased. Unionists who had lined the streets, waiting for hours to pay their respects on the day of Zola's funeral, clashed with police when a fellow member was threatened by a mounted policeman for singing the "Internationale." Even six years after Zola's death, outraged reactionaries and anti-Dreyfusards tried to block the transfer of his remains from Montmartre to the Panthéon, using manifestos, demonstrations, and, finally, violence. They failed and Zola was duly enshrined.

It was, of course, through his writings that Zola earned this passionate allegiance. His novels, classified as "naturalistic," were founded on large blocks of background material which had been diligently researched and scientifically observed. With this technique he created a long series of books based on the Rougon-Macquart family. The novels detailed, specifically, the rise of a peasant clan and, generally, the rise of the bourgeoisie. In these works Zola produced powerful social exposés, laying bare many of the sordid details of life and work among the lower classes. His stance was not political, but more that of an impartial observer convinced that wretched environments produced coarse lives marked by poverty, sickness, violence, and alcoholism. For this he won the admiration of unionists and reformers.

But Zola did not limit himself to social reform. From the start he was a staunch defender of Manet, boldly predicting in the face of ridicule that his paintings would one day hang in the Louvre. It is a wonderful example of poetic justice that Manet's portrait of Zola now hangs in that museum's Jeu de Paume gallery. A friend of Cézanne's from childhood, Zola was an early champion of other impressionists as well, though by the 1870s his support began to waver. He questioned whether their lack of success wasn't due, finally, to insufficient genius. The impressionists broke with Zola after the publication of his novel *L'Oeuvre*, whose central character, a talented but failed artist, was based on a composite of the impressionist circle.

Zola's greatest moment came with the writing of the tract "J'accuse," in defense of the Jewish army captain, Alfred Dreyfus. So strongly worded was "J'accuse" that the government was forced to bring two libel trials against Zola, leading to his self-imposed exile in England for almost a year. But the trials served their purpose. They helped to bring out the truth for which Zola had risked fines, imprisonment, exile, and even death from hostile crowds.

Three years later, in 1902, in good health and spirits and certain of the glowing future that science would bring, the man who Anatole France would call "a moment of the conscience of man" died of asphyxiation from a blocked chimney in his bedroom. The deathbed confession many years later of a laborer, who had been working on a nearby rooftop just before Zola died, raised suspicion that the blockage was a successful assassination attempt on Zola by the anti-Dreyfusards. But sufficient evidence did not exist to confirm it.

VICTOR HUGO b. *February 26, 1802, Besançon; d. May 18, 1885, Paris.* Victor Hugo was a bonfire that fed on everything in its path. The spark nearly went out several times as the sickly infant with the dwarfish look struggled for his life, but after that, problems such as his parents' discord and conflicts at school only fanned the flames. Tragedy and success alike made him stronger, and even the deaths of those close to him never made him miss a deadline. Somewhat embarrassingly, into his eighties, he still indulged his daily appetite for young girls. But by then he had buried his wife, Adele Foucher, four of his five children, and his mistress of 50 years, Juliette Drouet. He had also put to bed several million words of poetry and prose.

Everything about Hugo was larger than life. When he ran for political office he was soon raised to the Académie Française, then to the peerage. When he returned to Paris after 19 years of self-imposed exile (rather than live under Louis Napoléon's dictatorship), huge crowds greeted him, chanting their favorite lines from his works. Even when in the wrong he was quickly forgiven: surprised in a police raid instigated by her irate husband, Léonie d'Aunet was taken to Saint-Lazare prison and charged with adultery— while Hugo, invoking the inviolability of the peerage, went calmly home to bed. Madame Hugo took it less calmly, but she was used to his peccadillos and concentrated on basking in his reflected glow.

Hugo's glow came from the success of such novels as *Les Misérables, Toilers of the Sea,* and *The Hunchback of Notre Dame,* but his true literary worth may rest more on his poetry. Not as well known in America as the novels, it describes the universality of experience but with a certain banality, a weakness that caused André Gide to affirm that France's greatest poet was "Victor Hugo, alas."

During his lifetime he was treated like a god. He took up the plight of the impoverished and politically disenfranchised and backed up his words with substantial financial contributions. He also put on weekly luncheons for the poor children of the area, a gesture from which, it must be admitted, he gained considerable publicity.

When Hugo died of pneumonia at 83, his country threw itself into an orgy of mourning. He lay in state under the black-draped Arc de Triomphe while thousands trooped past. Two million Parisians trailed his coffin to the Panthéon. The cortege included orphans (who at the time were often invited to join in funeral processions) and devotees waving placards bearing their favorite Hugo titles, as if touting political candidates.

Even death could not completely put the bonfire out.

Marcelin Berthelot (1827–1907) and Louis Braille share the third cell. Berthelot, who first synthetically produced acetylene, ethyl alcohol, and benzene, was one of the fathers of modern organic chemistry. Braille, of course, has one of the most identifiable names in the world.

LOUIS BRAILLE *b. January 4, 1809, Coupvray; d. January 6, 1852, Paris.* Louis Braille comes close to being a candidate for sainthood. But like many who were later canonized, he was unrecognized during his own lifetime. He was known for his optimistic and generous nature, his musical gifts and his persistence in perfecting his system of reading by dots. Yet when he died at 43 of tuberculosis, there were no special observances and not even so much as a brief obituary in the newspapers. Braille was buried quietly at Coupvray in the parish churchyard.

One hundred years later came the scramble to locate his remains, place them in a double-sealed coffin, and enshrine him here. Only his hands, with which he perceived so much of life, were left in Coupvray, sealed in an urn. Leaders of the blind from all over the world gathered in Paris to acknowledge their debt to Braille.

Louis' blindness came from an accident when he was three years old. Playing in his father's harness shop, he plunged a sharp tool into his left eye. The wound was treated by a local herbalist with lily water, which stopped the bleeding but not the internal hemorrhaging. Louis spread the infection to his good eye by rubbing it, and within weeks he was totally blind.

But he was also fortunate. Louis had a father who continued to treat him normally, a village priest who insisted on educating him, and a young schoolmaster who made a special place in the classroom—unheard-of concessions in a time when the nonsighted were considered to be mentally defective and on occasion were sold to organ grinders.

At 10, through the influence of the village marquis, Louis was sent to Haüy's National Institute for the Blind in Paris. Bright and adventurous, he overcame his disappointment at the school's primitive conditions and vowed to somehow learn to read. He was discovered to be musically gifted, but it took the insistence of Cherubini for Braille to be given organ lessons. As an adult Braille played the organ in the leading churches of Paris.

Persistence and purity of vision were his life's motifs. He began as a very young man to devise a method of reading by interpreting symbols, moving from raised roman letters to various patterns of dots. He worked all his life to refine and promote his technique, but when he died in 1852 it was far from accepted. There were many different systems on the market, several by influential inventors with funds to promote them, and for a while the Braille method was lost in a welter of raised alphabets and various other symbols. It took nearly a hundred years for it—and its inventor—to emerge as the clear favorites.

The most notable occupant of the last alcove is **Jean Jaurès** (1859–1914), an extraordinarily gifted speaker and writer who was instrumental in the development of the Socialist party in France. On the eve of World War I, Jaurès, who had been calling for arbitration instead of fighting, was shot to death as he sat in the Café du Croissant. His assassin, aptly named Villain, was acquitted "for acting from patriotic motives."

CHAPTER 6

ST. ETIENNE-DU-MONT

▲   ▲   ▲

The last act is bloody, however brave be all the rest of the play; at the end they throw a little dirt upon your head and it's all over forever.

—BLAISE PASCAL

AFTER EMERGING FROM the Panthéon, walk across Place Sainte Geneviève to the Church of St. Etienne-du-Mont. A late Gothic edifice, it would be worth viewing even if Racine, Pascal, and Marat were not buried here. Across the front of the sanctuary is a delicately carved rood screen (ca. 1525) and a spiral staircase. On the right is an intricately carved pulpit under a wooden umbrellalike structure (ca. 1650), which is decorated with sculpted figures and an angel on the top. The stained-glass windows, beautifully decorated with complex scenes, were executed between 1550 and 1600.

Two-thirds of the way down on the right is a glass coffin with ornate brass decoration, said to hold the remains of Sainte Geneviève, patron saint of Paris. In A.D. 451, when Attila the Hun and his army had pillaged Cologne, deflowered eleven thousand virgins, and were then casting about for other worlds to conquer, Geneviève persuaded her fellow Parisians not to flee, promising them that God would save the city. At the last minute the barbarians attacked Orléans instead.

Though cynics maintained it was because Attila had found out that Paris was the last place on earth to look for eleven thousand virgins, Geneviève was credited with the save and formally made a saint in 1330. It is alleged that in the antireligious fervor of the Revolution her bones were removed and destroyed. Her coffin is, nonetheless, a suitable remembrance.

Those looking for other ornate tombs here will be disappointed. On either side of the Lady Chapel are simple columns where Racine and Pascal are buried opposite each other. If they knew it, they would no doubt feel honored. The Lady Chapel was one of the most coveted spots for interment and they were, after all, neither clerics nor kings:

JEAN RACINE *b. ca. December, 1639, La-Ferte-Milan; d. April 21, 1699, Port-Royal.* Like a surprising number of other illustrious men, Jean Racine lost his mother in infancy. By the age of four he was an orphan, raised first by his grandparents, then by his grandmother alone in a strict Jansenist stronghold, Port-Royal. This experience was one from which he never recovered.

Jansenism, a form of Catholicism, leaned heavily toward predestination and away from free will. It emphasized personal holiness in the mode of St. Augustine and opposed all pleasure for pleasure's sake. The theater was particularly condemned.

Unfortunately, that was the area in which Racine's gifts lay. He broke with Port-Royal when he was 24 to embark on a literary career, but he was not allowed to stray unnoticed. He received daily letters from former colleagues and family members—"excommunications," he called them—imploring him to see the error of his ways. His Jansenist teacher, Pierre Nicole, published a pointed polemic in which he characterized authors of novels and plays as "public poisoners of souls and spiritual murderers."

It was heavy ammunition. But Racine continued to sin by writing some of the most brilliant plays in French drama: *Phédre, Andromaque, Brittannicus,* and *Iphigenie.* He was a master of psychological realism and created wrenching and often murderous conflict. In his personal life he enjoyed love affairs with actresses Champmesle and du Parc.

Then suddenly his fling was over. At 38 he renounced the theater and reconciled with Port-Royal. He married, produced seven children, and became an official historiographer for Louis XIV—a post he took very seriously. With the exception of two commissioned religious dramas, *Esther* and *Athalie,* he never wrote another play; indeed, he cautioned his own son against novels, operas, and the theater and helped bully La Fontaine into renouncing his own worldly ways before he died.

At his request Racine was buried in the cemetery at Port-

Royal. Above his head the wrangling between the Jansenists and Jesuits continued until, in 1709, the Pope ordered the destruction of Port-Royal. Buildings were razed and the dead exhumed and reburied. And Paris, like an aging mistress, reached in and claimed her wandering playwright once again.

BLAISE PASCAL *b. June 19, 1623, Clarmont; d. August 19, 1662, Paris.* "All our arguing comes down to a surrender to emotion. The heart has its reasons that reason does not know," Pascal wrote in his *Pensées.* Admitting that fact did not deter Pascal in the least from his cerebral pursuits. From his precocious childhood on he pursued mathematics, science, invention, love, philosophy, and religion with a rare intensity and vigor, arguing all the way through his brief life.

Pascal's mother died when he was only three. He was raised along with his sisters, Gilberte and Jacqueline, by their devoted father, Etienne, who occupied a prominent tax post. More importantly, M. Pascal had a gifted mind and some very definite and unique views on education, views which a century later Rousseau might have found compatible. Scorning established schools, deferring rote learning in favor of reason and method, and supplementing his teachings with innovative educational games, Pascal's father saw his talented children flourish.

By the age of 13 Blaise was attending meetings of the prestigious Académie Libre (forerunner of the Académie des Sciences), of which his father was a member. At 16 he published his significant theory of conic sections, and at 20 he conceived of a mechanical calculator. Two years later he produced a working model for which he received international recognition. During the next several years he produced important monographs in physics on the existence of a vacuum, the equilibrium of liquids, and the weight of a mass of air.

During this time Pascal embraced Jansenism, an unyielding, fundamentalist form of Catholicism, and with the arrogant fervor of youth attacked poor St. Ange, a visionary priest. This passionate, overzealous attack served to ruin the good priest's career. Never having attended school, Pascal was short on socialization, and his approach to people was frequently arrogant and condescending, yet flavored by a wit and insight which ultimately charmed more than it repelled.

This dubious charm made Pascal a favorite in some wealthy circles. He, in turn, was seduced by his rich friends' money, and insouciant sophistication. Though not poor he could not hope to compete but, typically, he tried. For five years he played the dandy, experiencing sexual adventures, a love affair, and a glittering social life.

Eventually he became disenchanted and even embittered with the world of society. He furiously turned to work as an escape and produced his famous theory of numbers. But even work was not enough. Under continual religious pressure from within and without (his sister Jacqueline was now in a convent), his doubts continued and his despair increased.

On the night of November 23, 1654, Pascal experienced a mystical revelation of God that altered the course of his remaining years. He staunchly defended Jansenism and Arnaud, one of the sect's persecuted leaders, in his *Lettres Provinciales*. He wrote his famous *Apology* which was based on his *Pensées*. Abjuring the life of the flesh, he attempted saintliness.

But neither his body, long wracked with peritoneal tuberculosis, nor his temperament were suited to this lifestyle and his zealous work habits took their toll. In the end it was a life surrendered to the heart in passionate belief, but ever supported by rational argument.

The final inhabitant of note, a controversial personality with several last resting places, scarcely belongs in a church at all. Expelled from the Panthéon, he was reinterred in the churchyard outside. When that disappeared, he was placed where he remains at present—near the front, under a statue of "Mater Misericordie":

JEAN PAUL MARAT *b. May 24, 1743, Switzerland; d. July 13, 1793, Paris.* Marat captured public imagination, as fanatics often do. He was barely five feet tall with the torso of a wrestler and the legs of an invalid. His bony face did not attract affection, though it glowed with fiery purpose. Initially a scientist and a doctor with a prosperous practice, he carried the seeds of paranoia from the start; they sprang to life when he was refused membership in the Academy of Sciences. Marat truly believed that the Academy members who claimed to find his treatises mediocre, were actually terrified by his brilliance.

His journey to anarchy was a long one. When he first published his newspaper, *L'Ami du Peuple*, Marat was critical of the ministers of Louis XVI but not of the king himself. He still clung to the belief that he was a Royalist. But his denunciations of the Minister of Finance, Necker, and the Convention were taken as seditious and he was forced into hiding by threats of police arrest. Gradually he also became disillusioned with the King.

Marat hid in the cellars of friends not, as was popularly stated, in the sewers of Paris. The dampness exacerbated a skin disease, causing extreme irritation and itching, and he spent his waking hours in his bathtub trying to get relief. This soon-to-be-famous tub was built like a kayak with a discreet covering at his waist, so that he could respectably entertain. Louis XVI had been executed and the Girondins banished, but Marat was still anxious to sniff out treachery. So when Charlotte Corday arrived, hinting of Royalist plots in her native Caen, Marat trustingly invited her in.

Charlotte blamed most of the Revolution on Marat's incendiary writings and had read enough of them to know how to capture his interest. He asked for details of the plot and Charlotte gave him names of "Royalist conspirators." Marat assured her, "They will soon be guillotined," but that answer was not to her liking. She plunged a knife into his lung and he cried out, then died. Charlotte was immediately seized by his wife and neighbors.

Charlotte Corday flashes briefly across history, a momentary face in a crowd, before dropping back into darkness. A conservative idealist, her inspiration was the biblical Judith. In the four days between the murder and the day she was guillotined, she admitted wanting to be a martyr to "the cause of liberty."

That title, however, was given to Marat. He had correctly diagnosed his appeal to the masses as his ability to give a voice to their rage, and he was not forgotten by them in death. Children and towns were named after him and statues erected in his honor. His body lay in state until premature putrefaction from his skin disease made a quick burial necessary. A year and a half later, Jean Paul Marat was reburied in the Panthéon. The body of Mirabeau, his archenemy, was expelled at the same time.

Yet even enshrined he did not age well. Six months later, amid complaints about his early Royalist leanings and embarrassment over his fanatical outbursts, the Convention voted that recipients of "Panthéonization" had to be dead at least 10 years.

Marat was not grandfathered in.

CHAPTER 7

MONTMARTRE

▲ ▲ ▲

*My favorite walk, especially when
it is raining, when it is pouring
with rain, is through Montmartre
cemetery, which is near where I
live. I often go there and I have
many friends there.*

—HECTOR BERLIOZ

ONCE THE HOME of Renoir, Van Gogh, Utrillo, and
Picasso (who chose it primarily because the rents were
cheap), the neighborhood of Montmartre carries a special
charm. The area probably got its name from "Mons Mar-
tyrum" (Martyr's Mound), referring to St. Denis who in A.D.
285 and at the age of 90 was beheaded here. He preferred
to carry his head several miles to a place that became the
site of St. Denis Basilica, rather than risk burial on unconse-
crated ground.

Montmartre was next considered for burials around
1806. Although planned as a collection of underground
vaults, Cimetière du Nord as the cemetery was first known,
turned out to be similar to Montparnasse and Père Lachaise.
The main difference is that it is even more like a small city,
an impression enhanced by its two levels of mausoleums
set off against a backdrop of apartment buildings. For all
that, Montmartre is not an ugly cemetery, and many famous
people have selected it as their last residence.

To reach the 28 acres of Montmartre Cemetery, take the
Métro to Place Blanche and walk west on Boulevard de
Clichy, being careful not to miss the right turn onto Rue
Rachel, the second side street. The entry is impressive. On
the right is the monument to actors Lucien and Sacha

Opposite: Robert Didsbury's tomb

Guitry; on the left are several interesting tombs of the not-so-famous. As with the other cemeteries, we have listed only the divisions with prominent people or unusual monuments. Divisions 5 and 21 are particularly worth seeing.

DIVISION 1

In a spectacular location, the nicely landscaped tomb of **Lucien** (1860–1925) and **Sacha** (1885–1957) **Guitry**. A father-and-son theatrical combination, Lucien went for the understated gesture while Sacha favored the stern profile.

DIVISION 3

Writer **Théophile Gautier** (1811–1872), author of the brilliant novel *Mademoiselle de Maupin* and an outstanding poet to whom Baudelaire dedicated *Les Fleurs du Mal*. On his grave stands the muse of epic poetry, Calliope, who appears to be headed for dinner with a duck, a loaf of French bread, and his medallion under her arm.

DIVISION 4

In a mausoleum which has his face on the door and uses the family's affectation of "de Gas" to hint at nobility is a painter who didn't share his family's pretention:

EDGAR DEGAS *b. July 19, 1834, Paris; d. September 27, 1917, Paris.* When he was 59, Edgar Degas rather unceremoniously evicted the remains of a cousin from the family vault to make room for himself. Although he was not to need it for another 24 years—outliving such contemporaries as Manet, Pissarro, Toulouse-Lautrec, and Van Gogh—it was crucial to Degas that he stay in the neighborhood.

Degas was raised a few blocks away by cultured parents and, after briefly attending law school, persuaded his father to let him study art in Rome. For a long time he was an artist in search of a subject. Though his portraits of family members were impressive, he cast about for themes that would please the Salon judges, making pages of notes on the blinding of Oedipus and Mary Stuart's extradition from France. He actually painted such scenes as *Semiramis Building Babylon* and *The Daughter of Jephthah* (copying a horse from one ancient artist and a soldier from another).

But his integrity saved him from being a mere Salon *pompier* (the word, meaning fireman, allegedly came from the resemblance between the helmets of Roman warriors in academic paintings and the headgear of Parisian firemen). Degas worked constantly on new techniques and ways of seeing, experimented with the placement of his subjects (frequently off center), and ultimately developed his own special themes: laundresses, women bathing, the worlds of horse racing and ballet. As Francis Steegmuller points out, by his very mastery "Degas stands between subsequent artists and the ballet dancers and racehorses they might have wished to paint in ways of their own. Few artists have dared paint ballet dancers and racehorses since Degas." While he was not the only artist to discover the power of glowing colors and exquisite lines, his use of them assured his place in history.

In his personal life, Degas' passions ran on a very small track. He never married and never had any known love affairs, male or female. Although he sometimes rhapsodized on the joys of a home and family, he felt that such responsibilities diluted one's art. To his circle of friends, which included Berthe Morisot and Mary Cassatt as well as the impressionists and writers Ludovic Halévy and Emile Zola, he was considered ironic, harshly opinionated, but often kind.

In later years Degas became anti-Semitic, breaking off old friendships over the Dreyfus Affair. He developed other crotchets as well, scoffing at people he called "thinkers," insisting that all that mattered was "work, business, and the army," and commenting that outdoor landscape painters should be shot by the police. By then his own eyesight was failing and he had stopped working, leaving an emptiness

Kaminski, a Polish soldier

in his life that he could not fill. By the time he died of a cerebral hemorrhage at 83, he was ready to take his place in the family vault.

DIVISION 5

A full-sized statue of a melancholy maiden drops flowers on **Henri Mürger** (1822–1861), a writer who died at 39, never recovered from the poverty he described in *La Bohème*.

Two others in this section, unknown except as they are shown on their monuments, also died young. **Kaminski**, a Polish soldier killed in 1859, is buried under a striking sculpture which depicts the dying soldier with his head thrown back in agony, realistic even to the torn-open coat. Sixteen-year-old **Louise Thouret** (1852–1868) is sculpted in white marble and shown lying in bed, covers pulled up over her chest and a scroll falling from her limp fingers.

In contrast to these poignant portraits is the plain arched stone of the Vestris family. Argumentative and vain, ballet star **Gaetano Vestris** (1729–1808) was considered The God of Dance, a title he passed down to his son, **Auguste** (1760–1842).

Also buried in this section are **Adolph-Charles Adam** (1803–1856), composer of "O Holy Night" and **Paul Delaroche** (1797–1856), whose romantic yet classical style caused him to be labeled as "eclectic." His most famous painting is probably *Napoléon Crossing the Alps*.

(A) Zola family
(B) Hector Berlioz
(C) Jean Baptiste Greuze
(D) Heinrich Heine
(E) François Truffaut
(F) Théophile Gautier
(G) Alexandre Dumas fils
   Robert Didsbury
(H) Louise Thouret
(I) Edgar Degas
(J) Henri Mürger
(K) August Vestris
(M) Jean Foucault
(N) Jacques Offenbach
   Léo Delibes

(P) Charles Fourier
(Q) Vaslav Nijinsky
(R) Cavé family
(S) General Jomini
(T) Delphine Gay
(U) Goncourt brothers
(V) Stendhal
   Juliette Récamier
(W) André-Marie Ampère
(X) Bertrand Douvin
(Y) Nadia Boulanger
(Z) Alphonsine Plessis

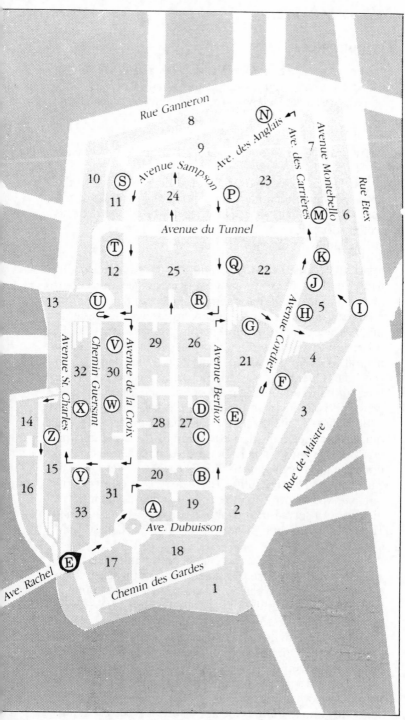

DIVISION 7

The bust of **Jean Bernard Léon Foucault** (1819–1868), the doctor who demonstrated the rotation of the earth, rests against a tall stele which lists his other achievements.

DIVISION 9

Two composers are within an orchestra's length of each other:

Léo Delibes (1836–1891) composed seriously for the French opera. The monument profiles him on its front and lists his works on its sides. He is actually best known for his ballets, *Coppélia* (1870) and *Sylvia* (1876).

In a family tomb with his bust on top is composer:

JACQUES OFFENBACH *b. June 20, 1819 Cologne; d. October 5, 1880, Paris.* An early workaholic, Jacques Offenbach's life proceeded at a tempo similar to that of his famous cancan. While not the life in the fast lane that his gout might lead some to believe, neither was it a strict life of sober industry. Blessed with a sharp eye for satire and a natural melodic gift which some felt rivaled Mozart's in potential, Offenbach was able to parlay his talents into a long and successful string of operas and operettas and provide his family with a comfortable lifestyle.

Born Jacob Offenbach in Cologne, Germany, he was quickly supplied a musical education by his father, an itinerant cantor and fiddler. Because of anti-Semitism and limited educational opportunities, he was taken at age 14 to Paris with his brother, Julius. There he so impressed Cherubini with his virtuosity on the cello that he was admitted to the Paris Conservatoire, despite its ban on foreign students. The boys made their living performing in choruses and orchestras.

It was at this time that he changed his name to Jacques and began to compose. His talents and enthusiasm soon gained him entry to important individuals, and commissions came his way. Touring with his cello he earned enough, including a jewel from Queen Victoria, to claim the hand of Hermaine d'Alcain, converting to Catholicism in the process. Offenbach's works gathered critical acclaim, but he continued to be snubbed by the Opéra-Comique.

Energy and talent would not let him lie low for long. He started his own company, Les Bouffes-Parisiennes, and so began his impact on the theater. Satire was his forte; and government, bureaucracy, and other composers (Gluck, Berlioz, and, most prominently, Meyerbeer) were his frequent targets. His spendthrift ways put him on the edge of disaster more than once, but his never-ceasing work pulled him through.

The Offenbachs were known for their soirées and Jacques for his loves, although it has been said that he was frequently in love but rarely a lover. An evening's entertainment might include family and friends performing musicals with Bizet at the piano and Offenbach and Halévy, his frequent librettist, in the leads. Other guests over the years included Nadar, Delibes, Doré, Maupassant, and both Dumas.

Offenbach's music is marked by a deceptively simple style. His lyrical melodies perform leaps of fifths or sevenths with such agility that the listener is unaware of their difficulties. Whether caught in the whirlpool of his own industry or simply lacking sufficient challenge, Offenbach did not fulfill his potential. But even Wagner, whose musical style and interests were far removed, praised Offenbach's melodic gift. It still charms today. The wit perseveres, and the sentiment of arias such as Perichole's letter song and the "Barcarolle" from *The Tales of Hoffman* are affecting without being cloying. Although he didn't live to see it performed, it was in this last work that Offenbach approached the mastery of which many thought him capable.

DIVISION 11

General **Henri de Jomini** (1779–1869), a Swiss soldier and military strategist who served under Napoléon, then defected to the Russian army—and lived to tell about it.

DIVISION 12

In adjoining tombs are **Delphine Gay** (1804–1855), a beautiful and witty novelist who ran a distinguished salon, and her husband, publisher and writer **Emile de Girardin** (1806–1881). Their inscriptions read, "Death has separated us. Death has reunited us."

DIVISION 13

Jules (1830–1870) and **Edmond** (1822–1896) **Goncourt**, literary brothers. Although the 26 years between their deaths makes the bronze cutout profiles lying on the tomb look like father and son, the Goncourts collaborated closely on novels, art criticism, and a journal about their contemporaries. Edmond also donated the celebrated Prix Goncourt which is awarded yearly to an outstanding work of French prose.

DIVISION 15

Alphonsine Plessis is also known as Marguerite Gautier (1824–1847), the patron saint of unrequited love. Although in real life she was engaged to a count, she did die tragically of tuberculosis in Alexandre Dumas fil's arms—inspiring him to write *La Dame aux Camélias* with its closing lines, "Sleep in peace, Marguerite. Much will be forgiven you because you greatly loved." (Verdi also based *La Traviata* on her story.)

Something about the beautiful young courtesan who carried white camellias 25 days of the month and red the other 3, still touches the hearts of young women. Her simple stone monument, with its enameled pillow reading "Regrets," is always covered with flowers.

DIVISION 18

Pierre Alexis Ponson du Terrail (1829–1871), one of the earliest mystery writers, whose serialized exploits of his character Rocambole helped sell French newspapers and entertained Manet on his deathbed.

DIVISION 19

Mme Alexandre (1839–1925), **Dr. Marguerite** (1891–1962), and **Dr. Jacques Zola** (1891–1963). Zola himself was, of course, moved to the Panthéon, but his wife and two children by his mistress are still here, watched over by his brooding countenance.

DIVISION 20

This section holds the simple black monument, marked with his trademark, of the very colorful composer:

HECTOR BERLIOZ *b. December 11, 1803, La Côte-Saint-Andre; d. March 8, 1869, Paris.* If Hector Berlioz were alive today, his behavior would be labeled obsessive-compulsive by clinicians; but that would take all the fun out of it. He was the quintessential romantic, a man given to extremes of emotion and for whom half-hearted opinions did not exist. With a great shock of reddish brown hair topping his intense hawklike features, his appearance matched his temperament. And like a hawk, little escaped his notice. His exquisite sensitivity invariably resulted in passionate outbursts. On more than one occasion his midperformance opinions thundered through the concert hall. "Not two flutes, you wretches—two piccolos! two piccolos!"

Berlioz was an example of the rare composer who cannot play the piano. Raised in the town of his birth, he was only mildly encouraged in his musical studies. Never was the parental eye cast towards music as a career. Medicine was to be Hector's profession, chosen by his physician father. In due course he attended medical school, but the charnal house stench of the dissecting room and the lure of music were too strong. Moving to the Paris Conservatoire, he quickly made up ground while retaining the unorthodoxy of the self-taught. He was revolutionary. His harmonies and modulations were new, and his ear for color and orchestration were unmatched. His use of themes foreshadowed Wagner's idea of leitmotivs. Berlioz reveled in the idea of a large orchestra and fully utilized all its color and power to express his heightened emotional messages.

Music was his medium, but love was at the core of his life. His first love, at age 12, was Estelle Duboeuf. She was 18 and barely knew he existed. His most famous love was Harriet Smithson, the Irish actress, with whom he fell in love at a distance. He terrified her with his ardent love letters and a visit to a rehearsal where, upon finding her in the arms of an actor, he let out a shriek and fled the hall. She became the beloved, the idée fixe in his famous *Symphonie Fantas-*

tique, which depicts the hallucinatory hell his love puts him through; it includes her participation in a mocking, orgiastic dance at a witches' Sabbath.

Several years were to pass before they met again. In the interim, Berlioz was spurned by another woman. Not without a sense of humor, at least in retrospect, Berlioz described in his wonderful *Memoirs* how, in close succession, he vengefully plotted her murder (he was to gain entrance to her house disguised as a chambermaid), attempted suicide (a passerby rescued him from drowning), then, drained of his passion, he spent the three happiest weeks of his life in Nice. He eventually married Harriet in 1833, but within five years, spurred by her drinking and his romantic yearnings, he found love in the arms of the lovely Marie Recio Martin, an aspiring opera singer with a voice like a cat's. They lived together for years, finally marrying seven months after Harriet died in 1854. Marie died eight years later.

The two women were united when Harriet's remains were moved from the smaller Montmartre cemetery before it was razed. Berlioz, there for the exhumation, described how the gravedigger "with his two hands picked up the head, already parted from the body. . .[and then] gathered in his arms the headless trunk and limbs, a blackish mass which the shroud still clung to. . . ." And so Berlioz had his last encounter of the fantastique with his Harriet.

At age 60, lonely and tired of life, Berlioz still pursued his romantic obsessions. He attempted to renew his very first love affair, making a pilgrimage to his old summer home to renew the sensations of his childhood love and then going on to see Estelle. Cordial, but not reciprocating his love, she did allow an occasional visit, and letters passed between them. For Berlioz it was a solace which saw him through to the end.

DIVISION 21

This elongated section is actually on two levels. Walking along Avenue Berlioz from the entrance, you first see, on the right, the plain black marble tomb of filmmaker **François Truffaut** (1932–1984), whose innovations pointed the way to New Wave cinema. Starting out as a factory worker, Truffaut became an important film critic, was drafted into the army, deserted, and finally began making movies. He produced such well-loved films as *The 400 Blows* (1959), *Jules and Jim* (1961) and *The Wild Child* (1970). His inscription reads, *La terre te cache mais mon coeur te voit toujours* (The earth covers you but my heart will see you always).

Along here also is the monument of artist **Jean-Honoré Fragonard** (1732–1806) whose rococo style of plump cupids and diaphanous garments is currently out of vogue. He died at 74 while eating ice cream.

If you climb the stairs toward the back of the division, you will reach the monument of **Robert Didsbury** (1890–1910). Little is known about him except that his statue, portraying a woman in gauze, head thrown back in sorrow, was sculpted by his grieving mother.

Not far away is the white marble gisant which, from the front, appears to be all feet, that of:

ALEXANDRE DUMAS fils b. *July 27, 1824, Paris; d. November 27, 1895, Paris.* The fils (meaning "son of"), always tagged to the end of his name like a tin can on the tail of a cat, branded Alexandre as the afterthought of a more successful father. Until he was six he lived with his mother, Catherine Labay, and was largely ignored by his famous father. Then Dumas père, in a fit of conscience, went to court to establish paternity and, after a custody battle, brought Alexandre to live with him and his latest mistress. When that did not work out, the unhappy child was sentenced by the Court to boarding school.

Dumas fils, more withdrawn because of his early unhappiness, lacked his father's boisterous joie de vivre but copied Dumas père's extravagant lifestyle and love affairs. They allegedly shared mistresses and traded boasts; to someone who commiserated with him over having such a father, Alexandre answered, "At least, if he doesn't set me a good example, he provides me with an excellent excuse."

Alexandre also wanted to write (though his father tried to discourage him, grumbling that if he had had any inkling beforehand he would never have allowed his son to share his father's name). The son produced 13 forgettable novels and some bad poetry before his successful *La Dame aux Camélias*. Several other successful plays followed, including a rather pointed one, *The Prodigal Father*, in 1859.

Ultimately Alexandre turned from a profligate life, made sure his mother was comfortably settled in a sunny apartment, then married a Russian princess, Nadezhda Naryskine, who had already given him two daughters. Generous and sociable, though with a cutting wit, Alexandre was elected to the Académie Française before his father and given the Legion of Honor. He died at 71 of meningitis complicated by an embolism, believing that he had redeemed the tag-along status with which fate had burdened him.

Yet, rather unfairly, most of his plays died with him. And

Cécile Firman, an unknown

standing at his marble gisant, it is hard not to think of *The Three Musketeers* and *The Count of Monte Cristo* as the true Dumas legacy. The old reprobate who wrote them is buried northeast of Paris in Villers-Cotterets.

Right next to it is the striking tomb of a **Laver-Frantz**, about whom we have no biographical information. It is guarded by two Egyptianate creatures with women's faces and pointed breasts, and the flanks of wolfhounds.

DIVISION 22

Laure Junot (Duchess d'Abrantes, 1784–1838), wife of General Junot. Originally a childhood friend of Napoléon, she eventually cast her lot with the Royalists, causing him to exile her from Paris. But she found a sweet revenge. After his death she wrote her *Memoirs*, which included highly suspect conversations in which he poured out his soul to her, and for which she received an enormous amount of money.

Also in this section, under a plain arched stone which gives his name and that of Serge Lifar who arranged his reburial here, is the immortal dancer:

VASLAV NIJINSKY b. *March 12, 1888, Kiev; d. April 7, 1950, London.* If the term idiot savant had not fallen into disrepute, it would be a perfect description of Vaslav Nijinsky, a dancer some believe to have been the greatest of this century. Born in Russia to theatrical parents, Vaslav was a poor student with an unremarkable personality. But even as a boy at the Imperial School of Ballet he could leap higher and stay airborne longer than anyone else. And it was, in part, a personality like an empty mirror that enabled him to totally become Narcissus, Petrushka, and the other character roles he danced.

After graduation in 1909, Vaslav began performing with Sergei Diaghilev's Russian Ballet Company. His position in the company and in Diaghilev's heart allowed him to choreograph a number of ballets as well, including Debussy's *L'Après-midi d'un Faune* and Stravinsky's *Le Sacre du Printemps*. Although these efforts got mixed reviews, his performing was universally praised as brilliant.

But outside the world of the theater, his childishness was obvious. Although seemingly content as Diaghilev's captive lover, the first time he was apart from Diaghilev on a tour to South America, he became engaged to a woman he scarcely knew. They could barely communicate (he spoke only Russian, she French), but he married Romola de Pulsky in Buenos Aires in 1913. Naively, he expected Diaghilev's blessing. What he got instead was the full force of his mentor's fury and a telegram advising him that his services as a dancer would no longer be required. Nijinsky indignantly resigned instead. But it was a disasterous move. Severed from the company which had given his life meaning, he danced only a few more times before sinking into schizophrenia, a condition that would last the rest of his life.

That fateful marriage, impulsive on Nijinsky's part, was not at all so on Romola's. After seeing him dance in 1912 she was determined to have him, and she systematically attached herself to Diaghilev's company, making sure that her cabin was near Vaslav's when they sailed for South America.

Certainly she did not expect to ruin her husband's career, although, as she knew Diaghilev, she might have anticipated his violent reaction. In any case, neither rival knew what losing the company would do to the dancer. When a stricken Diaghilev tried to restore Vaslav, it was already too late.

For 30 years Romola sought cures and supported the wounded dancer while raising their two daughters, a life she certainly had not foreseen. After Nijinsky died of kidney failure in 1950, she wrote candidly about the man who, in less docile moments, had tried to push her down stairs and off cliffs. But there must have been better times, or else she was exceptionally forgiving, for after his death she also wrote, "You were privileged among so many millions of women to share his life, to serve him. God gave him to you. He has taken him back."

Vaslav was given a substantial funeral and buried in St. Marylebone Cemetery outside London. But three years later, when Romola was in America, another dancer, Serge Lifar, arranged with Vaslav's sister to have him exhumed and reburied in Montmartre, near Auguste Vestris and in the city where Nijinsky had had his brief hour of triumph.

DIVISION 23

Charles Fourier (1772–1832), a social philosopher who advocated dividing society into self-supporting communities or "phalanxes." Brook Farm in West Roxbury, Massachusetts, was only one of a number of communes inspired by his works. Engraved on a plain stone tomb surrounded by black iron railings is one of his tenets, *Les Attractions sont proportionelle aux destinées* (The attractions are proportional to their destinies).

DIVISION 25

On Avenue de Montmorency in this section is the mausoleum of **Cavé**, an engineer, and his family. Its blue-painted iron doors show scenes of a shipwreck with the Angel of Death hovering around the prow, possibly signaling his interest in naval engineering.

DIVISION 27

Jean Baptiste Greuze (1725–1805), an artist whose favorite subjects were buxom but unhappy young girls (e.g. *Young Girl Weeping Over her Dead Bird*) and the genre known as Beautiful Deaths which generally showed a dying patriarch surrounded by his family and servants.

In later years Greuze was surrounded by a coterie of young women who had artistic aspirations; one is even sculpted standing disconsolately on his tomb, eyes lowered, basket under her arm. The words on the monument erected by his "daughters" translate "He painted virtue, friendship and innocence, and his soul breathes through his pictures."

Above a flower-covered lyre, head bowed as if napping, is the bust of Heinrich Heine. The poem on the base, inscribed in German, is far from one of his best. It lacks the bitter irony which contrasted so effectively with his lyric style. Nevertheless, the last verse gives a strong hint of his simple elegance and graceful imagery.

Who knows where, fatigued with straying,
Where my final rest will be?
In the South, where palms are swaying?
Underneath a linden tree?

Shall a desert be my host,
Buried by a stranger's hand?
Or along some ocean coast
Shall I slumber in the sand?

Still, God's sky will be my cover
There as here; and every night
Overhead the stars will hover:
Lamps to give the dead their light.

Trans. by Aaron Kramer

HEINRICH HEINE *b. December 13, 1797, Dusseldorf; d. February 17, 1856, Paris.*

> A lonely fir tree is standing
> On a northern barren height;
> It sleeps, and the ice and snow drift
> Cast round it a garment of white.
>
> It dreams of a slender palm tree,
> Which far in the Eastern land
> Beside a precipice scorching
> In silent sorrow doth stand.
>
> Trans. by E. A. Bowring

Written early in his life as an expression of unrequited love for a cousin, this poem is also prophetic and revelatory in its depiction of the dilemma of thesis and antithesis in Heine's life as well as the ever-elusive synthesis. It is a statement tinged with the bitter irony which underlay his yearning for unity in his undertakings. Only in his poetry did he come close to resolving this problem, and then only in form. His poems were songs without music. No other poetry has lent itself so readily to music. More than three thousand musical settings, including some by Schubert, Schumann, and Liszt, attest to his facility with lyric form.

Heine's feelings were often marked by passionate ambivalence. He loved his native Germany, believed in its potential, but despised its authoritarian instincts and its harsh treatment of Jews. Born into that religion he forsook it as a young man and became a "baptised Jew," a Christian in name. He did this so that he might practice law, a profession then banned to Jews. Such expediency was not uncommon, for many professions were prohibited to Jews. Heine struggled with the problem of religion all his life, at times bitterly abjuring both faiths and, for a period, favoring the idealistic pantheism of Saint-Simon and his philosophy of human progress.

Neither could Heine find equilibrium in love. In turn, his two pretty, wealthy, and intelligent cousins spurned his love. Eventually he settled for the safety of a young shop girl, Mathilde Mirat. Immature, flighty, and nowhere near his intellectual equal, she nonetheless delighted him with her childlike enthusiasm and devotion. Still, she was never the woman of his love poems who aroused such passion and bitterness as:

> My songs are poisoned say you—
> How could they wholesome be
> When my young blood is tainted
> With a poison poured by thee?

A fervid admirer of the ideals that inspired the French Revolution, Heine attacked the abuses of the aristocracy in Germany and earned the status of persona non grata. Though not officially exiled, he left his beloved country and, from age 18 on, spent most of his years in Paris. With his genius, handsome looks, and ironic wit, he quickly gained entry to the highest intellectual circles. He flirted with George Sand and made the acquaintance of Chopin, Berlioz, Dumas, Balzac, and Marx. His flippancy often masked his true passions and offended many who thought him merely brash and superficial. His poetry and prose emphatically proved otherwise. His political writings, many of them biting satires, continued to center on abuses of personal liberties, especially in Germany, but he angered many of his fellow expatriates by refusing partisan alignments.

Heine married Mathilde in 1841. By then he was almost blind, probably a result of syphilis. He suffered a gradual paralysis of the face and, as his body gave way, he spent his last eight years on his "mattress grave." Throughout this tortuous ordeal he worked, entertained visitors, and retained his famed wit. Holding up a paralysed eyelid in order to see the dim outline of a visitor, he remarked that "Alexander Weill came to see me. We exchanged ideas, and now I'm utterly stupid." Or, as his nurse easily lifted his husk of a body to the window for a view, he quipped, "See how the people of Paris carry me on their shoulders!" On his deathbed he threatened to refer God to the Society for the Prevention of Cruelty to Animals and assured Mathilde that God would pardon him because that was His job.

Again it was black humor; wit designed to cover the pain of his fate and that of much of mankind. But the bitter irony belies the jokes, and his writings show that he faced life with courage and portrayed it with clarity. His life and ideals never achieved synthesis, but he never surrendered. He was a writer to the end. In his pained and veiled world, his last words were "Paper and pencil!"

DIVISION 28

Pauline Viardot-Garcia (1821–1910), daughter of tenor Manuel Garcia. Her voice was described by Saint-Saëns as "pungent, like the taste of a bitter orange, made for tragedy or epic verse"; and though her voice failed her in middle age, she remained a fascinating woman. For many years she was Ivan Turgenev's lover.

DIVISION 29

Martin Charcot (1825–1893), noted neurologist whose works on hysteria and hypnotism influenced Sigmund Freud. His son, **Jean Baptiste Charcot** (1867–1936), also buried here, was an antarctic explorer as well as a neurologist. He made seven trips to Greenland to collect scientific data aboard his ship the *Pourquoi Pas?* before crashing into a reef off the coast of Iceland.

DIVISION 30

André Marie Ampère (1775–1836), the physicist who formulated the theory of electrodynamics and who had the amp (unit of electrical current) named after him. He lies in a grave with his bronze profile above it.

Several yards away, under a very plain stone monument with the words *Priez Pour Eux* (Pray for them) on it, are philosopher **Pierre Simon Ballanche** (1776–1847), his life-long friend Juliette Récamier, and her parents.

JULIETTE RÉCAMIER *b. December 4, 1777, Lyons; d. 1849, Paris.* In this simple grave lies what is left of the most beautiful woman in Paris—at least so considered during her lifetime. The most famous portrait of Mme Récamier is by David, showing her in her perennial white gown with puffed sleeves, dark curls in place, reposing on her chaise lounge.

Juliette's beauty was not illuminated by intellect. Nor was she sensual. Although she was married at 15 and was involved in romantic intrigues all her life, her marriage was never consumated, and her lifelong virginity was a fact, not a disguise. The point at which she might have weakened was the year she turned 40 and became involved with the writer Chateaubriand. But when he requested some proof of her affection she fled the country and didn't return until, as she wrote, she felt their relationship could be "as calm as a good conscience and pure as virtue."

In any case, Juliette was the only woman in Paris who could keep a fashionable salon going simply by looking beautiful.

Finally, in a grave with a shape similar to Ampère's, also displaying a bronze profile, is the writer:

STENDHAL (Marie Henri Beyle) *b. January 23, 1793, Grenoble; d. March 23, 1842, Paris.* A contemporary of Stendhal's once quipped that the author's two lasting regrets were that "he was fat and squat and would have liked to be delicate and slender, and that he had been born a commoner and could not console himself for not belonging to the nobility." Stendhal himself might have added that he would have preferred that his mother had not died in childbirth when he was seven—and that she had not been buried with a full panoply of morbid rites which left him terrified of death ever after.

Losing his beloved mother left him with a permanent legacy of isolation from the world. Later on he attempted to fill her place with numerous affairs; but in childhood he contented himself with an unreasoning hatred for his father who, though rigid and bourgeois, certainly cherished his son. But Stendhal was unrelenting. This early scorn for authority equipped him as an adult to take on both the Church and society.

He had some insight into his own character, of course, realizing early that nothing could really satisfy him. At 23, living with the actress Louason (Mélanie Guilbert), he reflected, "I passionately wanted to be loved by a woman who was melancholy, thin, and an actress. I have been, and I haven't found continual happiness." Although he had at first considered Melanie "sublime," he soon convinced himself of her lack of intelligence and continued to search ephemerally for the great love of his life. Most of his affairs were with married women (making a permanent commitment impossible), but he proposed to a great many others and was always turned down.

During his lifetime Stendhal disgorged a great mass of material, including travel stories, literary and political analysis, art criticism, a biography of Rossini, and novels, two of which are considered his masterpieces: *The Red and the Black* in 1830 (red for the Army, black for the Church), and *The Charterhouse of Parma* (1839). When these books came out they were widely read and widely criticized for their unflattering pictures of society. They were also criticized for details—such as a heroine's kissing a severed head—which polite society found repugnant. Stendhal did not have a way with words or great plotting skills, but he was able to focus on telling human detail and portray the psychology behind the action. He created a bridge to the modern novel.

Stendhal contracted syphilis in Milan at 19, but, unlike other of his contemporaries, his case was not terminal. He died instead of a stroke at 59, a well-known writer, but relatively unmourned. In contrast to the thousands that usually joined the cortege of a famous person, only three friends followed his coffin to Montmartre. And instead of being buried in Rome beside Shelley as he had wanted, he was laid to rest at the rear of the cemetery, in the shadow of the viaduct bridge.

Yet after he died something interesting happened. His rather wavering reputation thickened and took root. In 1905 a committee was formed to erect a memorial to him, with a sculpture by Rodin based on a medallion by David d'Angers. As he took his place in literature, cemetery officials evidently reconsidered his treatment; in 1962 he was moved out of the viaduct's shadow and finally placed in the sunshine of the main road.

DIVISION 32

Bertrand Douvin (1933–1954), a pilot who—briefly—held the world record for duration of flight. His jaunty face, framed by a wreath, appears under a fascinating sculpture of a huge wing.

DIVISION 33

We conclude with a flower-carved tomb in the shape of a church window, that of an important musical family whose leading light was:

NADIA BOULANGER *b. September 16, 1887, Paris; d. October 22, 1979, Paris.* Nadia Boulanger (meaning "baker" in English) earned her fame primarily as an influential teacher of music. Her critics felt she merely produced an endless row of students baked in the neoclassical mold. But for most students and observers she was a dominant force in twentieth-century music. A first-class lecturer, she was able to convey the intricacies of music with unusual clarity and enthusiasm. Many students who observed her class were captivated and enrolled eagerly. She demanded and provided an extraordinary degree of dedication, knowledge, and imagination. According to Alida Lessard, a former student, she "saw the harmonic system as a moral system and mixed up hell and damnation with parallel fifths."

Because of the strong pro-American feeling in France after World War I, many Americans were drawn to Paris to study, specifically to the Conservatoire Américain, where Nadia taught. She was an admirer of Gershwin and of the improvisatory nature of jazz, and she was a strong believer in the emergence of American music. It was with her American students that she developed the informal but selective following known as the "Boulangerie." Her influence on American music can be found in the music and performances of Aaron Copland, Roy Harris, Walter Piston, Elliot Carter, David Diamond, and, in later years, Quincy Jones and Julius Katchen.

Boulanger's influence on the continent's music scene was similarly impressive. She studied with Fauré and became one of the chief exponents of his famous *Requiem*. She greatly admired and espoused the works of Stravinsky, who was her good friend and fellow teacher. Her European students included Igor Markevitch, Jean Francaix, Lennox Berkely, Dinu Lipatti, and Clifford Curzon.

Nadia's domineering perfectionism stemmed from her upbringing. Her mother, extremely strict, was a firm believer in controlled development. As a child Nadia was tied to a chair to improve her posture (always ramrod straight as an adult), and rigorous intellectual demands were placed upon her. Although she progressed rapidly, she never satisfied her mother; as talented as Nadia was, she suffered in comparison with her younger sister, Lili, who demonstrated even greater precocity in musical endeavors. Until her mother's death in 1935, Nadia lived under her domineering influence, simultaneously extending similar demands on those around her.

In her adolescent and early adult years Nadia developed her talents as a composer, pianist, organist, and conductor. Although clearly one of the most gifted of her generation, she still had to fight against sexual prejudice. She had to overcome Saint-Saën's opposition to win the second prize in composition in the prestigious Prix de Rome competition. She fought hard to gain the respect of the orchestras she conducted. She was, in effect, an early feminist, although more in deed than in political philosophy.

Through all her varied roles—teacher, composer, conductor, and performer—the same traits were evident: a sense of self-discipline which bordered on the self-destructive, an autocratic and frequently insulting attitude toward her students, an obsessive sense of the loyalty due her and music, and an intense sense of privacy regarding her own feelings. Away from work she was warm and funny, taking a passionate interest in the lives of her students. Their reminiscences are fond, for her concern and devotion could not be doubted. But a student's early departure equalled desertion. Music came first. The trivial, such as marriage, came second. For several years she sent black-bordered notes to a former student on the occasion of her wedding anniversary.

Boulanger demanded most from herself. Despite failing sight, crippling arthritis, and numerous infections that increasingly affected her in old age, she continued to teach with the same all-consuming dedication. By her ninetieth birthday even this was not enough. Her body had all but given way, and she was experiencing more frequent periods of confusion. Yet music still permeated her world. In speaking with her shortly before her death, Leonard Bernstein discovered that she still heard music in her mind. Curious, he asked which of her favorite composers she heard. She replied "A music that has neither beginning nor end."

Also buried here are Nadia's mother and her sister, **Lili** (1893–1918), who was the first woman ever to win the Prix de Rome for musical composition. She displayed the same hard-driven dedication to music as Nadia's, composing up to her death despite intense pain caused by ulcerative colitis. Her output was slight because of her early death. Clearly a great promise was denied. Lili Boulanger's music is still played occasionally, and several of her works have been recorded.

CHAPTER 8

ST. VINCENT

▲   ▲   ▲

Death opens the gate of fame
and shuts the gate of envy.
—LAURENCE STERNE

A PLEASANT CODA to a Montmartre Cemetery visit would be a stop at St. Vincent, a delightful cemetery the size of a sheet cake. Although only a handful of its inhabitants are famous—Maurice Utrillo, Arthur Honegger, and Théophile Steinlen—it contains some of the most surprising statuary in Paris, including a dollhouse with faces peeking out.

To reach St. Vincent from Montmartre, walk up Rue Caulaincourt or take the Métro to the Lamarck stop and ascend to Place Pequier. Cross Rue Caulaincourt and make a sharp left into the tiny Rue Lucien-Gaulard, where the cemetery entrance is nearly hidden from view. The statue of the man and woman embracing chastely in the Place Pequier is a monument to artist **Théophile Steinlen** (1859–1923) who was originally buried inside the cemetery. He is best-remembered for his early advertising posters and witty sketches of cats.

Because of its tiny size, St. Vincent is not divided into sections. In describing its monuments we have taken an easily followed circular route. Immediately on entering the cemetery you will see a large monument of a lamenting muse carved into a large flat stone, her arm extended up to indicate the mustachioed, fedora-capped occupant, **Faria** (d. 1911). From a distance the stained weathering gives the woman the look of a flapper; the sculpting by Charpentier was done, however, in 1912.

Close by is the grave of **René** and **Jean Dumesnil**, which depicts two women in graceful poses atop a large tomb. They are looking fondly at each other, their left hands brushing in farewell, for one is earthbound and the other already ascending.

Across the path but still on the main road is the tomb of the composer **Arthur Honegger** (1892–1955). Honegger was a Swiss composer who maintained his allegiance to Switzerland even though he spent much of his life in France. Although he was a member of that loosely knit group of French composers known as Les Six (see Poulenc) and was socially close to them, Honegger's own musical style was predominantly influenced by German music.

He experimented with many forms, including jazz and Gregorian chants, and was greatly influenced by Bach's chorales. His most popular piece was the tone poem "Pacific 231," based on his impression of a steam engine. He wrote many operas and experimented with vocal techniques including screaming, whispering, and speaking in addition to the usual singing. Honegger's works, while interesting, are not often heard today.

Harry Baur (1880–1943), a well-known actor, is buried under a simple black tomb on the corner of the next path. Baur began on the stage, then imprinted his strong personality on European cinema. He played the composer in *The Lives and Loves of Beethoven* and starred in *Les Misérables*, *Crime and Punishment*, and many other films. Baur's career was cut short by World War II, when he was arrested and accused of being an Allied agent. Imprisoned in France and tortured by the Gestapo, he was eventually released but died mysteriously a few days later.

Continuing to the next corner, we find a remarkable sculpting for the **Bussoz** family. It is done in a style reminiscent of Rockwell Kent's and portrays with great simplicity and feeling a young boy with large angel wings. He is quietly seated, hands clasped in front and head bowed in sorrow.

Moving up the path beside the outer wall we first pass the monument of the **Defradas** family, the headstone detailing two ancient Greeks. Then, at the base of the stairs, we come to what would be a nondescript modern tomb except for a woman in classical dress standing to the right of the headstone. She appears to have wandered up from the Defradas grave. The juxtaposition is bizarre, but so was the life of the artist buried here.

MAURICE UTRILLO *b. December 26, 1883, Paris; d. December 6, 1955, Dax.* The geometric, rather pastel streets and houses that Utrillo painted, with their always-exact perspective, scarcely give a hint of the unlovely child who grew

into an emotionally disturbed adult. Ironically his mother, Suzanne Valadon, was probably a better artist. She was more skillful in her use of color to create a mood, and when Degas saw her adolescent drawings he pronounced her "one of us!"

Although Toulouse-Lautrec was Suzanne's lover, the father of Maurice was Adrian Boissy, an insurance clerk turned painter and heavy drinker. However, when Maurice was eight, his mother decided that Boissy was not worthy of her son and persuaded a Spanish journalist, Miguel y Molins, to adopt him. The new father's duties included giving Maurice his family's name, Utrillo, though not actually raising him or supporting him financially.

It was surprising that y Molins agreed even to that. Maurice was a moody child, instinctively shunned by others. His grandmother gave him *charbrol* (a peasant broth containing wine) to calm him, and by 16 he was a full-blown alcoholic. Suzanne, belatedly realizing the problem, sent him to Sainte Anne's, a hospital-asylum. It was to be the first of many similiar confinements.

At his discharge from Sainte Anne's the doctors suggested art as therapy, a suggestion Suzanne resisted. But when Maurice came home and spent hours just staring out the window, she began to teach him. From the beginning he was content to paint the streets around him, never tiring of doing the same ones over and over. He soon learned to do a painting, then slip out and barter it for a night of drinking. Very often he picked a fight in the bar and found himself arrested for assault.

Utrillo's attitude toward women, even when sober, was bizarre. If he found himself alone in the street with one, he would tremble all over with rage, start yelling threats, then chase her down the block (though he carefully never caught her). Pregnant women especially incensed him. Utrillo was well-known by the citizens of Montmartre, and eventually he was not allowed on the streets without a paid attendant. A violation meant a return to Sainte Anne's.

In or out of the hospital, Maurice continued to paint prolifically. He lived with his mother (whom he revered along with the Virgin Mary and Joan of Arc) and her husband, André Utter, who was Maurice's age. By 1919 prices for his work had begun to soar, though money meant little to him. He was happy with a few toys—electric trains and children's musical instruments—and enough watered-down red wine to get him through the day. He still had to be chaperoned in public and watched for a tendency to expose himself, announcing, "I paint with this!"

Surprisingly—though more through a transfer of custody than a courtship—in 1935 Maurice married an enterprising widow, Lucie Valore. By then Suzanne Valadon was in poor health (she was to die three years later from a heart attack); Utter had left her for another woman.

In 1955, a short time before Utrillo's own death from pneumonia, the Musée National de l'Art Moderne put on a retrospective of his paintings. Knowing he could not tolerate other people, he was invited to a private premiere and shown through 50 years of his life. Impassively he walked through his youth, then suddenly stopped before a painting from the years he called his White Period and broke into tears. "Despite everything, how beautiful it was," he sobbed.

Appropriately, just above his monument we can glimpse the rooftop of *Le Lapin Agile* (The Nimble Rabbit), a café which Utrillo frequented.

Retracing our steps to the second path which cuts across the cemetery and turning left, we come to one of the most imaginative and appealing monuments of all, that of **Platon** and **Papuoe Argyriades**. At first our eyes seem to deceive us. We can't believe that what we are seeing is a house. Yet the peaked roof is covered with Spanish tiles, and beneath it is a wooden window frame. Painted on the windows are green curtains, and peering out beneath them are a husband and wife who appear to be in their thirties.

ICI REPOSE
MAMAN PERDON
- Infirmière Major 1914-18
Chev. Légion d'Honneur
6 DÉC. 1872 - 30 NOV. 1954

Their portraits are done in a relaxed, informal style which is utterly charming. He takes on a mysterious air for we see only half of his face; the other half is hidden by part of the frame. She wears a black dress with a white lace collar; up close we can see that her mouth is painted in the shape of a small heart. On either side of the headstone are two planters, and in front is a raised area for plantings. The effect is that of a married couple looking out over their garden to see who has come to visit them.

Back uphill and on the right is still another exceptional monument in this small cemetery, this one belonging to **Maman Perdon** (1872–1954), a nurse major in World War I. The modern bas relief on the headstone is eloquent in its portrayal of this determined woman. Pinned on the front of her habit are the numerous medals she won for her devoted service.

In the rear, just to the right of the central abutment, are the graves of the painter **Louis Carrier Belleuse** (1848–1913) and his wife.

Last on the downward trek is the small plot honoring another painter, **Georges Rose**. Here on a small palette half-hidden by ivy are the artist's name and dates; behind it is a clump of tall rose bushes perpetuating his name.

Bussoz family memorial

CHAPTER 9

LES INVALIDES

▲ ▲ ▲

Every man meets his Waterloo at last.

—WENDELL PHILLIPS

EVEN IF YOU think you don't like Napoléon, you should still visit Les Invalides. Despite the bad press he has endured over the years, Napoléon remains an enigmatic and fascinating personality—and one certainly deserving of a second opinion. The Dômes des Invalides is not solely dedicated to him, but to other military heros as well.

Although people might assume Napoléon built this cathedral for himself, it was actually begun in 1675 and finished in 1706, intended as a royal chapel for the Church of St. Louis (from which it is separated by a sheet of clear glass). Napoléon did believe it should be a military panthéon and brought the remains of Turenne here on September 21, 1800, but he had more ambitious plans for himself. He wanted to be buried along with his descendents in St. Denis, and in 1806 he ordered a burial vault there. The order was never filled.

To reach Hôtel des Invalides you can use either Varenne, Ecole Militaire, or St. François Xavier Métro stops. First you will need to buy a ticket in the flat building to the left of the Dôme's entrance. The ticket will also admit you to the Museum of the Army.

On entering Les Invalides' dome, you will pass statues of Charlemagne and St. Louis, then see a series of alcoves around the perimeter and a large circle in the center. If you can, resist looking over the circle's rim for the moment and start with the alcove on the right.

This chapel holds the simple black-and-white marble coffin of **Joseph Bonaparte** (1768–1844), Napoléon's older brother. Joseph, who was originally trained for the priest-

Opposite: Tomb of Ferdinand Foch

hood, became a lawyer. But when Napoléon assumed the emperorship and established a "royal line of succession," Joseph wanted to be included too. Napoléon made him the King of Naples and then of Spain. His reign was short-lived. Forced to abdicate in 1813 by other European powers, he moved to the United States and lived in Bordentown, New Jersey, for the next 26 years. He returned to Italy three years before he died.

From here go to the chapel just to the left of the entrance, that of Napoléon's other (and favorite) brother, **Jérôme Bonaparte** (1784–1860), represented by a black statue of himself above an ornate tomb. Handsome, high-spirited—and not a little spoiled, as the youngest of eight children—Jérôme joined the French navy but jumped ship in America to marry Baltimore beauty Elizabeth Patterson. Because Jérôme was still a minor, Napoléon imperiously had the marriage annulled and married the truant to Catherine of Württemberg instead.

In consolation, Napoléon brought Jérôme into the line of royal succession, giving him the kingdom of Westphalia (a province of Prussia) to rule. Jérôme ruled with zest. He effected a number of positive changes, but he was better known as The Merry Monarch because of his lavish entertaining and his generous gifts to his ministers. When Napoléon's empire was collapsing, Jérôme gave up Westphalia without a struggle and purchased a magnificent chateau in France. After Waterloo Jérôme left France, returning in 1847 and receiving a place of honor in his nephew Napoléon III's court.

The rest of the alcoves are filled with military heroes unrelated to Napoléon. If you head right again, past the alcove of Joseph Napoléon, you will see the monument of an early soldier, **Vauchon**, who died in 1707, an ornate white marble creation showing the general surrounded by desolate mourners.

Next to it is the most impressive tomb upstairs, particularly when seen from a distance, that of **Ferdinand Foch** (1851–1929). Created by Paul Landowski, it portrays eight dark military figures bearing the coffin aloft on their shoulders. A talented general, Foch helped to halt the German advance at the Marne in 1914 and later led the British, French, and American armies to victory in 1918.

Continuing past the altar and around, you come next to the chapel which holds the gilt-decorated black marble coffin of **Louis Lyautey** (1854–1934). Lyautey, a career officer, served mainly in Morocco, developing the economy, protecting its territory, and holding down tribal attacks on the sultanate.

The monument of **Henri de la Tour d'Auvergne**, (Vicomte de Turenne, 1611–1675) is a mirror image of Vauchon's, which it directly faces. The first occupant of Les Invalides, Turenne is one of France's greatest generals. The Thirty Years War gave him ample opportunity to hone his military skills and his strategies of using mobility and surprise attack. He died in battle in the Dutch Wars.

If you haven't done so already, look now over the rim of the circle and see the shining wooden sarcophagus of **Napoléon Bonaparte** (1769–1821). The sheer size of it (43 feet by 21 feet by 48 feet high) is stunning, a coffin fit for a Gargantua or Goliath rather than a 5'6" Corsican. Designed by Louis Visconti for a competition, it won over such contenders as a 20-foot statue of Napoléon atop a 50-foot pyramid and other, more flowery, types of funeary.

Like a set of Russian nesting dolls, there are six smaller boxes inside the purplish porphyry coffin—one of oak, one mahogany, two lead, one ebony, one tin—the smallest holding Napoléon. There was no doubt some significance in the number and kinds of materials used, but writer Rudolph Chelminski suggests another reason: "There is a minority of Parisians, those who are not affected by la Gloire, who will tell you that the real reason for the sevenfold boxing job is to make sure that he never gets out again."

Using the steps behind the altar, next descend to the tomb itself. **Henri Bertrand**, faithful general of Napoléon who was with him on St. Helena; and **Geraud Duroc**, one of Napoléon's closest aides, who died in the Battle of Bautzen in 1813, are buried outside the entrance. The lintel carries the Emperor's words, "Let me be buried on the banks of the Seine, near the people whom I loved so much." Around the tomb, in white marble, are 10 bas reliefs representing Napoléon's domestic achievements while in office and 12 figures which symbolize his military victories.

But Napoléon's impressive domestic reforms, which are often overlooked in favor of his battles, still didn't get him buried with kings. He had no children by Josephine, whom he subsequently divorced for political reasons, and his only legitimate son by Princess Marie Louise, **Napoléon II**, nicknamed King of Rome by his parents, is buried in the alcove at the foot of his tomb. The Empress, who fled back to her native Austria with her child after Napoléon's exile, feared the boy's brightness, feeling that "Precocious children don't live long." Indeed, Napoléon II died of tuberculosis at 21. His remains were brought to Paris in 1940 by the Germans and reinterred in Les Invalides in 1969.

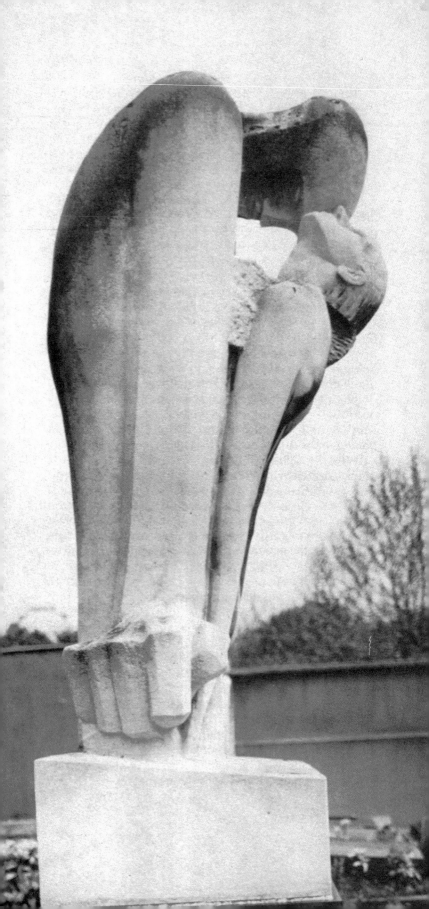

CHAPTER 10

PASSY

▲   ▲   ▲

*Death is only a larger kind of
going abroad.*

—SAMUEL BUTLER

RESTING IN THE shadow of the Eiffel Tower, the inhabitants of Passy have tombs with a view. Manet and Debussy are its most famous residents, but the cemetery has an interesting collection of aviators' graves and some startling sculpture as well. Covering only three acres, it can easily be combined with a visit to *Musée de l'Homme, Art Moderne*, or the Eiffel Tower.

The entrance is to be found on the Rue du Commandant Schloessing (Métro:Trocadéro). Although the cemetery is not officially divided into sections, we have numbered various areas on the map in an effort to facilitate touring.

DIVISION 1

Immediately on your left are three tombs which are worthy of attention. The first is a large concrete monument of modern design which swoops low in the rear. The heavy-looking door and the bas relief of one angel kneeling beside another are in sharp contrast, however, for theirs is a style of a much earlier age. The effect is curiously anachronistic.

Next is the tomb of the **Dupont** family, proprietors of the Dupont cafés. Under a roof supported by four columns is a statue of Mercury. Beside the Duponts, but less assuming, is the grave of the **Montcocol** family, which bears on its headstone a finely wrought angel, hovering with wings and arms outstretched. From even a short distance the effect is that of a butterfly, providing a sense of lightness and delicacy.

Opposite: Tomb of Antoine Cierplikowski

Tomb behind M. Bashkirtseff's grave

DIVISION 2

Rising above all its neighbors is the immense mausoleum devoted to **Marie Bashkirtseff** (1860–1884). The stained-glass window in back shows a palette, giving a clue to the resident's occupation. Marie, the daughter of a Russian emigré, was a briliant adolescent who lusted after life in all its guises. When she died at 24, she had managed to fill 84 volumes of a diary with passionate observations and candid descriptions of the famous people she knew personally. It was published posthumously, to the consternation of many who were unflatteringly described.

Marie also studied art and was recognized as a promising painter. Most of her work went to the Russian Museum at St. Petersburg. She died of tuberculosis in a white-draped drawing room, insisting, "I shall find something pleasurable even in death."

HENRY FARMAN
26 Mai 1874   17 Juillet 1958

Behind Marie Bashkirtseff and slightly to the right is a cherub seated on a block of stone at the foot of a small grave. Although looking away from the tomb, he is pointing back toward the cross which is resting on the headstone. His white stone contrasts sharply with the darkness all around him.

DIVISION 3

This division provides a glimpse of **Henry Farman** (1874–1958), a pioneer of aviation, shown at the controls of one of his early craft. In 1906 he won the Deutsch-Archdeacon prize of 50,000F. ($10,000) for being the first man to make a circular flight of one kilometer. In 1908 he made the first flight in a heavier-than-air craft over New York City. Farman went on to design and manufacture planes just outside Paris and created the first prototype for passenger airlines.

Turning around from Farman and walking just a short distance, you can see Dunikowski's powerful sculpting which marks the tomb of **Antoine Cierplikowski**, a minor painter of the 1920s who would otherwise have been forgotten. Here the joined bodies of a man and a woman press dramatically upward from the pedestal, his head bowed toward her uplifted face. Inscribed on the pedestal is the verse: *Je tends les bras vers l'infini, J'offre mon front a las lumière, Je rentre en la clarté première, et que le Maître soit beni*! (I stretch my arms toward infinity, I offer my face to the stars, I enter in the first light, that the Master be blessed!)

No matter what angle it is viewed from, its impact remains strong. This is one of the most impressive monuments in Paris.

PASSY

A Dupont family
  Montcocol family
B Marie Bashkirtseff
C Henry Farman
D Antoine Cierplikowski
E Jean Giraudoux
F Emmanuel de Las Cases
G Volterra family
H Maurice Bellonte
I Edouard Manet
  Berthe Morisot

J Réjane
K Trouselle family
L Jane Henriot
M Gabriel Fauré
N Claude Debussy
P Fernandel
Q Octave Mirbeau
  Dieudonné Costes

In the corner is the tomb of dramatist **Jean Giraudoux** (1882–1944) best known for his plays *Siegfried* (1928) and *The Madwoman of Chaillot* (1943).

Continuing along the wall we find a tomb topped with a small obelisk. It belongs to **Emanuel de Las Cases** (1766–1842), the historian and friend of Napoléon who shared his exile on St. Helena. To this friend Napoléon dictated some of his memoirs, which were published along with Las Cases' observations as the *Mémorial de Saint-Hélène*. While the work was originally thought authentic by historians of Napoléon, it is now viewed as an intimate but flawed account, albeit still worth reading.

Moving back along the road we come to the intersection which separates Divisions 5 and 6. Going either left or right here will provide a look at two interesting monuments.

Through the ages stone has been the chosen material to perpetuate the memory of the deceased. However, perhaps reminded of decay by Shelley's "Ozymandias," the creator of the next tomb took preservation one step further. Here we find a replica of Michaelangelo's *Pieta* encased in a plexiglass housing. The effect is curiously sterile, for one of the great appeals of cemeteries is that they show their age: tombs range from the shiny new to the weathered old. Death in a bubble seems no more appealing than life in one.

In contrast is a large metal casting, long turned green, of a dog faithfully resting in wait on his master's tomb.

DIVISION 6

On the road between Divisions 6 and 7 is a memorial to the **Volterra** family, listing several war dead. At the head of the tomb are metal castings of a young shepherd tending his sheep and, on the left, of a girl kneeling and strewing flowers above a bed of real flowers. The mood of pastoral quiet is particularly effective in this urban setting.

DIVISION 7

Just across the way is the tomb of **Maurice Bellonte** (1896–1984) who, with Dieudonné Costes, made the first east-west crossing of the North Atlantic in 1930 in a plane they called *Point d'Interrogation* (Question Mark). Symbolising Bellonte's early flights is Delannoy's artistic casting showing a courageous and determined Icarus flying above the sun.

DIVISION 9

Section 8 holds little of interest except the plain stone tomb with a multitude of fake flowers of the actress **Réjane** (1857–1920) who appeared in England and New York as well as in Paris. But across from 8, in Division 9 on the circle, is perhaps the strangest, most poignant monument in the cemetery, that of the **José del Saz Caballero** family. It shows a child of about five with bangs, wearing a frilly bonnet and clutching the sash of her old-fashioned dress. Is she merging with the pile of stones behind her, or emerging from them in a message of hope? Whatever the case, the effect is startling.

Next to her is the tomb of two noted artists and their spouses. Under the bust of Edouard Manet is also buried his wife, **Suzanne Leenhoff**, his brother, **Eugène Manet**, and Eugène's wife, painter Berthe Morisot.

EDOUARD MANET b. *January 23, 1832, Paris; d. April 30, 1883, Paris.* If ever a leader of a revolution was dragged into it unwillingly, stuffed into uniform and pushed into battle, it was Manet. Far from wanting to change the world, the tall, ginger-bearded artist, womanizer, and man about town wanted only the medals and awards of the Salon. He yearned for an acceptance that would make his fortune and quiet his parents' doubts about his chosen career. Certainly he knew that he could paint "Salon pictures." What he never counted on was his own integrity getting in the way.

To please his parents, as a teenager Manet joined a naval expedition to Brazil. But he was not cut out for life at sea. After his return his father consented to his studying art, and

Manet joined the studio of Thomas Couture. There he learned the rules of art. Painting, even of outdoor scenes, was to go on only inside the studio, with nude models (whose clothing was later painted on), elaborate props, and plaster casts. The artist was not permitted to have a personal vision or style; noble subjects were de rigeur. Manet, amused, poked fun at these conventions. Couture coolly demanded that he leave, and he did.

Manet's first submission to the Salon in 1859, *The Absinthe Drinker*, compromised by crossing Couture's under-

José del Saz Caballero family tomb

painting technique with a disreputable-looking junk dealer. The Salon didn't buy it. More cautiously, Manet submitted portraits of his parents and of a Spanish guitarist (the latest Parisian fad) to the Salon of 1861; when they were accepted, he felt that his future was assured. But his submissions in 1863, including the now-famous *Le Déjeuner sur l'Herbe*, which pictures two nude women in the woods with two dressed men, were roundly rejected. That particular painting was branded "obscene" by the critics.

Worse was to come. His *Olympia*, a nude reclining on a couch, was panned in the press as "a sort of female gorilla" and "putrefying . . . as if at the morgue." His art was shrilly condemned in reviews as daubs, excrement, "canvases for which no words are too bad." Each work that he exhibited privately brought forth further howls, as if he were deliberately trying to insult France. It made him the most famous painter in Paris, but hardly in the way he had anticipated.

By then, however, art had become its own reward. He rose at dawn, eager for another new day of painting, and at dusk headed for the Café de Bade or Tortoni's, where he held court among younger artists and writers. Besides having strong opinions about art, he was down-to-earth and witty. Whenever he met *Figaro* art critic Albert Wolff, who had finally admitted in print that Manet had "pointed the path to other artists," Manet would stand with his arms outstretched like a signpost.

Edouard's early personal life was also a compromise. He had gone home obediently to his parents every night, never letting on that he was the secret lover of Dutch piano teacher Suzanne Leenhoff and the father of her baby son. Though he and Suzanne later married and raised Léon, Manet never told his only child about his parentage. By the time the father felt able to do it, Léon was an adult.

The finally liberated Manet also had an eye (and often more) for beautiful women. Even when very ill, he always revived temporarily when one entered his studio. Suzanne took his philandering in stride though one day, seeing him in pursuit of a young woman, she overtook him. "This time I've caught you!"

"I thought it was you!" Manet replied cheerfully, and they both roared with laughter.

Sadly, the good times ended before Manet was ready. The poison of syphilis, which he traced to a carnival night in Rio when he was a teenager, crept through his body, affecting his left leg first. He fought the disease vainly with hydrotherapy, rest, and other cures. It seemed to him desperately unfair, when he was finally gaining a measure of Salon acceptance, to have to leave it all behind. (He had finally won a second class medal from the Salon that should have been given to him years before.)

Yet in 51 years the reluctant soldier had helped win the battle; though he had been the target of criticism for refusing to show his work in impressionist-sponsored exhibits he had, by holding out for official acceptance, opened wide the Salon doors for everyone. Nine years before his death he had a bookplate designed for himself with a Latin pun on his name, *Manet et manebit* (He endures and will endure). The words were more prophetic than his jeering critics could ever have guessed.

BERTHE MORISOT (Manet) *b. 1841, Paris; d. 1895, Paris.* Berthe Morisot was, unfortunately, married to the wrong brother. She did meet Edouard first, when she was a beautiful 27-year-old with luminous green eyes, white skin and black curls. They fell in love when she was posing for *Le Balcon*—the first of 10 paintings Manet did of her. But Manet was married. Berthe, an artist in her own right and a descendent of Fragonard, was too proud to be anyone's mistress.

Even though her work was lighter and more impressionistic than Manet's, Berthe had no trouble being accepted into the Salon exhibits. She favored a linear look, with subtle colors and white on white, and helped convert Manet to the pleasures of painting outdoors. She was more forward-looking than he and appears to have been happy in her work and her circle of friends.

But Mme Morisot, although she had encouraged her daughters to become artists, was even more anxious to see them safely married. Edma, Berthe's sister, had obliged her by marrying in 1868, and Mme pressured Berthe to accept Edouard's brother, Eugène, a lawyer. Though she considered him "three quarters mad," she convinced Berthe that a marriage with some "sacrifices" was better than having no status in life at all.

So in 1874 Berthe allowed herself to be led to the altar, and for the next 18 years she endured what everyone agreed was a difficult marriage. She still had her art, of course. But she never allowed her brother-in-law to paint her again.

DIVISION 11

In this division is the plain black stone tomb with a raised cross of **Fernandel** (1903–1971), the popular French film actor. Behind it, in the farthest corner, are a trio of interesting mausoleums, although nothing is known of the people who lie within them. That of the **Trouselle** family contains an amazing stained-glass window. While its colors are biblical, the people illustrated are dressed in contemporary (nineteenth-century) clothing. To the right, the chapel of **Compertz** is richly decorated inside with a Byzantine Christ in gold. And to the left is what one would imagine a Victorian mausoleum to be. On the exterior is a weeping cupid holding a death's head, directly over a painted window of two dismal cherubs in all-brown tints.

DIVISION 12

Across the way in this section is a tall stele topped with the bust of a strikingly pretty young woman wreathed in flowers. This is the grave of **Jane Henriot** (1875–1900), a young Comédie Française actress who died in a fire. Her inscription reads: *Elle est venue, Elle a souri, Elle a passé* (She came, she smiled, she left).

Also in this section is the flat rose stone of composer:

GABRIEL FAURÉ *b. May 12, 1845, Paniers; d. November 4, 1924, Paris.* Gabriel Fauré's musical talents came first to the attention of an old blind woman who heard the young boy playing the harmonium in a school chapel. She spoke to his father, the school's director, as did a friend later on, who advised enrolling the boy at the recently established Ecole Niedermeyer in Paris. It was a fortunate choice. His early studies were steeped in church music dating back to plainsong, but, more importantly, he studied under Saint-Saëns, only 10 years his senior and anxious to expose his students to the extracurricular music of composers such as Schumann, Liszt, and Wagner. Thus he developed an original and eclectic style that the more prestigious but conservative Paris Conservatoire might not have provided.

Fauré married (unhappily) and had two sons. An expert organist, he supported his family by playing in churches and giving lessons. Because his wages were low and remuneration from his compositions slight, he found time to compose only during summer vacations. His reputation developed slowly and finally gained ascendancy after he turned 40. His songs, which rank among the best ever composed, drew attention: their style is intimate, almost sparse, reflecting his study of early church music, but he was inventive in his harmonies and had a wonderful ear for melody. His music, which strongly influenced Debussy, has a subtle, refined beauty which reflects the gentle nature of the man.

In 1905 Fauré became the director of the Paris Conservatoire. Firm in his musical beliefs, he sought to bring innovation and life to a school entrenched in conservative methods and ideas. The old guard resisted the man they viewed as a Robespierre, but Fauré persevered, and, in a steady stream, the old guard resigned. The school took on new life and an enhanced reputation, as the success of its pupils attests: Ravel, Enesco, Roger-Ducasse, and Nadia and Lili Boulanger. Fauré retired in 1920 but continued to compose and achieved some of his finest works despite his declining health and increasing deafness. In old age his handsome features were complimented by an air of serenity and a lack of pretension, which made him immensely attractive. Unaffected by fame, he shared his time and advice with the younger generation. The members of Les Six were avid Fauré admirers.

His most famous piece remains his *Requiem*. Whether written for his father or "just for the pleasure of it," the music stands as a reminder of the simplicity and serenity of its composer.

DIVISION 13

In a plain black tomb with his name etched in gold is another composer:

CLAUDE ACHILLE DEBUSSY *b. August 22, 1862, St. Germaine-en-Laye; d. March 25, 1918, Paris.* Claude Debussy could be likened to a mythological creature. His pallid, overweight body took the shape of a corpulent circus bear, his bearded face and huge head caused him once to be described as a hydrocephalic Christ, and his eyes, according to Colette, were "like those of animals of prey." Feline in personality, he was independent, aloof, and self-centered. Indeed, he often seemed to prefer the company of his Angora cats to that of people. Most of his friendships seemed superficial, and even when they were not he could end them at the slightest question of divided loyalties. But whatever his appearance and idiosyncrasies, Debussy was a revolutionary composer who is now believed to have laid the foundation for much of twentieth-century music.

Controversy has surrounded Debussy's origins. Was he the child of Manuel and Victorine Debussy, keepers of a meager china shop, or did they agree to raise an out-of-wedlock child of the wealthy and cultured Achille Arosa and Madame Roustan (Manuel's sister, who took the name of Octavie de la Ferronnière to match her lover's social standing)? In any case, it was the frequent time spent with Arosa that exposed young Claude to the world of the arts. Arosa arranged and paid for his piano lessons with Mme Maute, a student of Chopin's (the same Mme Maute who approved, to her later regret, the marriage of her daughter to the poet Paul Verlaine). She brought out the boy's talent, and Claude was admitted to the Paris Conservatoire at the age of 10.

Formal studies and academic rules held little interest for the young Debussy, and he frequently annoyed and exasperated his teachers by his persistent challenging of accepted methods. He preferred to experiment; when asked, "But what rules do you follow?" he replied, "My pleasure, my whim." His pianistic studies lagged. Nevertheless, in composition he won the prestigious Prix de Rome though, typically, he could not tolerate the social demands that living with other winners at the villa in Rome entailed. He threatened suicide on bended knee before the astonished director and was allowed to leave before the two years of study were completed.

His early influences were Wagner and then Moussorgsky. The Russian influence stemmed from the time he spent as a house musician for Mme von Meck, Tchaikovsky's famous lover by letter. Moussorgsky's influence remained, but it was in the famous Paris café, the Chat Noir, that he met Eric Satie whose irreverent humor, and audacious music and esthetic attracted Debussy. The quirky Satie claimed that it was he who suggested to Debussy the idea of musical impressionism as a counterpart to the already established art movement and a furthering of a French style. "We ought to have our own music—if possible without choucroute."

Whatever Satie's influence, Debussy developed a style so opposed to Wagner's that not even a hint of sausage or sauerkraut remained. He disdained traditional forms and revelled in unresolved harmonies. In opera and song he felt that the music should serve emotion rather than create it, and that dramatic arias were unnatural and false. His music often consists of a delicate wash of tone and harmony meant to create an impression. His works such as *L'Après-midi d'un Faune* and *Jeux* did much to alter accepted notions of form and harmony and helped to break apart the traditional use of tonal music.

Debussy treated the first two women in his life badly. For years Gaby kept his house and protected his privacy, but she was ultimately turned out for her friend Lily. Upon their break, Gaby shot herself. Debussy coolly told his friends that she had merely been hospitalized. Although loving and loyal, Lily, whom he married, was dropped for Emma Bardac. Lily also shot herself (both women survived). Because Debussy's friends sided with Lily he could not forgive them, and most of his friendships were severed.

In Mme Bardac he finally found an intellectual and cultural equal. She was also monied; Debussy was often accused of marrying her for this reason. A daughter, Chou-chou, was born, and Debussy doted on her. If he ever truly loved anyone it was undoubtedly this precocious daughter, who died of diptheria at 13, only a year after her father. The famous *Children's Corner Suite* is dedicated to Chouchou.

Debussy died of cancer of the colon after years of suffer-ing. As the cortege carried him through the half-deserted streets of war-torn Paris, the loneliness of the procession, accompanied only by a few remaining friends, echoed the emotional barrenness of his life.

DIVISION 14

In our last section are two graves of interest, side-by-side. The first, that of **Octave Mirbeau** (1850–1917), is conven-tionally decorated with a bust of the author (now turned green) which does not hint at the passions of his life. An outspoken revolutionary and journalist, Mirbeau was con-stantly challenged to duels by those he insulted. Plays such as *Les Affaires Sont les Affaires* (Business Is Business, 1903) attacked the social order, but even when his novels weren't political, such as *Le Journal d'une Femme de Chambre* (Diary of a Chambermaid) his tone is vivid and intense. When he grew tired of fighting duels, he retreated to his estate at Cheverchemont where he died. His body was brought back to Paris to be buried.

The other grave is the newer, but striking and beautiful monument of the aviator **Dieudonné Costes** (1896–1973). The headstone contains two adjacent medallions colorfully depicting the western and eastern hemispheres. Above them is a billowy third medallion showing a bright red biplane in flight. On the right medallion, radiating from Paris, are silver rays reaching to various global points to which the aviator flew. The Eiffel Tower, rising up to the left of the grave, provides an air of history which makes it easy to imagine a solo flier departing from Paris on a foggy night in the dangerous early days of flight.

CHAPTER 11

ST. GERMAIN-DES-PRÉS

▲ ▲ ▲

When a whirlwind has blown the dust of the churchyard into the Church and the man sweeps out the dust of the Church into the churchyard, who will undertake to sift those dusts again and to pronounce, 'This is the Patrician. . .this is the Plebian?'

—JOHN DONNE

ST. GERMAIN-DES-PRÉS, LOCATED near the traditional hangouts of Left Bank artists and writers (and across from Café des Deux Magots), is the oldest church in Paris. Built over a Benedictine Abbey (ca. 558), it dates from the eleventh and twelfth centuries and retains traces of Romanesque influence. Inside, the nave is brightened by the frescoes of **Hippolyte Flandrin** (1809–1864) whose bust guards them, and by the ceiling which is painted a deep blue with gold stars. The church was originally designated as the burial place of royalty, but even its founder, Childebert I, was moved to St. Denis around 1263. Three other great men, Mabillon, Boileau, and Descartes, are still here.

How did they merit being buried inside a church? In the beginning that was an honor reserved for religious personalities, kings, and wealthy donors. Then great men were ocasionally permitted, and well-off craftsmen and tradesmen began creeping in—as did those directly connected to the cathedral, such as the architect. Pierre de Montreuil (d. 1267), who designed St. Germain-des-Prés rests here under a plaque which describes him as a "perfect flower of good morals, in his lifetime a doctor in stone."

The most desirable spot was under the choir near the altar; next was the Lady Chapel (the one dedicated to the Virgin Mary) or under the pew where the family sat. When the ground under the flagstones became too crowded, the older bones were moved up into the attic to make way for new burials. The poor but faithful were buried out in the churchyard in a common trench.

The inevitable happened, of course. First there was just the hint of an odor emanating from the increasingly crooked flagstones; then people began to notice that the bones in the churchyards were no longer staying underground. Finally in 1776 Louis XVI forbade the burial in churches of all but religious figures, and this law was strengthened in 1804 when all church burials were forbidden. The offending bones had already been carted off to the Catacombs, and Père Lachaise was scheduled to open in 1804 to receive the newer dead. Fortunately for our purposes, the bones here were left intact.

To tour St. Germain, enter in back and start down the far left aisle. In the first chapel that you come to, St. Xavier's, is the mausoleum of **John Casimir** (d. 1672), King of Poland and head abbot of St. Germain. Just beyond is the tomb of **William Douglas** (d. 1611), tenth Earl of Angus, who served under Henri IV.

In the next niche, the chapel of St. Peter and St. Paul, is a plaque commemorating **Nicolas Boileau** (1636–1711), a poet who participated in round-table dinners several times a week with Racine, La Fontaine, and Molière. Boileau made his reputation from his literary criticism and from his satires, especially *Le Lutrin* (The Lectern, 1683) and *Satire II* (1662). Epicurean and highly sociable, Boileau held his love of mimicry just enough in check to be buried in church.

By looking directly across to the right, you can look up and see the bust of **Jean Mabillon** (1623–1707) highlighting the chapel of St. Benoit. Mabillon, a Benedictine monk, was the first to concern himself with the authenticity of ancient documents and scientific methods of judging their age. In this chapel are also buried **Montfaucon** (1655–1741), another Benedictine monk, who through his study of antiquities is considered one of the founders of modern archeology. Here, too, is noted philosopher:

RENÉ DESCARTES b. *March 31,1596, LaHaye; d. February 11, 1650, Stockholm.* It is natural to assume that the bust dominating this chapel is that of Descartes. But in a city which has immortalized even the unknown soldier in stone, no recognized statue of the philosopher exists. Fortunately he was painted a number of times, so we are able to picture him as a dark-haired, striking-looking man with a moustache, a tiny triangular beard, and broken nose.

In his portraits he gazes out with the curious detachment he brought to life itself. After his mother died when he was an infant, he never grew close to his father, brother, or sister. He did have a six-year involvement with a Dutch servant girl, Helen, and fathered a daughter, Francine, but he never acknowledged them to anyone. Their existence has been pieced together from cryptic notes in his diary and from public documents. When Francine died at age five of scarlet fever, Helen disappeared from his life as well. Thereafter his relationships with women were platonic.

Although of a later century, Descartes ("I think, therefore I am") was truly a Renaissance man. In addition to his philosophy, which sought to prove the existence of God, the measurable reality of the physical world, and the validity of human reason, Descartes composed music, originated analytical geometry, developed the law of optical refraction, and pioneered in anatomy, botany, psychology, and medicine.

Although Descartes had few close friendships he was widely admired, and when he died at 53 of pneumonia there was a struggle over where he would be buried. He had been in residence in Sweden at the invitation of Queen Christina, and she wanted to inter him in an elaborate monument in Stockholm's largest church. But his Catholic

colleagues objected to his burial in a Protestant church and interred him with a Catholic service instead. Descartes' monument in Stockholm was a simple stone with comments in Latin summarizing his achievements.

As his works posthumously increased in popularity, the French began to clamor for his body's return, and finally in 1666 Sweden agreed to let him go—but not before his coffin, waiting for safe transport, had been looted for holy relics (fingers, teeth, etc.) by his followers. From Copenhagen the remains were transported by land to avoid their being pirated at sea by the admiring English. Yet even in Paris his traveling was not over. His body spent time in Eglise de Sainte-Geneviève, and then in Lenoir's Museum of French Monuments, before it was moved to St. Germain-des-Prés in 1819.

Or what was left of it was moved. The skull that housed the brain that once extolled public creativity and personal privacy is now naked to view in Paris' Musée de l'Homme.

To finish the tour, continue past the altar and up the right side to the chapel which holds **Lord James Douglas** (d. 1645), a Scotsman in the employ of Louis XIII. Beyond the door are the tombs of brothers **Olivier** (d.1664) and **Louis** (d.1669) **de Castellane**. Both died fighting for Louis XIV; their statuary is by François Girardon.

In the garden outside are fragments of sculpture from around 1250, the time of Pierre de Montreuil.

CHAPTER 12

THE CATACOMBS

▲ ▲ ▲

*And some there be that have no
memorial. Their bodies
are buried in peace but their
name liveth forever more.*

—ECCLESIASTICUS

ALTHOUGH AN IMPORTANT part of Parisian funerary history, a visit to the Catacombs is not a good choice for the squeamish or claustrophobic. You descend round and round, down stone steps in a narrow spiral until you begin to sense what eternity is all about. At the bottom, the main attraction seems to be endless walls of tibias and skulls arranged artistically amid quotations about death. Yet such caveats aside, the Catacombs have a fascination all their own.

The Municipal Ossuary was a former gypsum quarry, and, unlike the Roman Catacombs where the early Christians met secretly, it was not even consecrated for burial use until April 7, 1786. Immediately after that date, bones from the notorious Cimetière des Innocents were transferred here. Other overcrowded churchyards soon followed suit. At dusk the bones were loaded into carts, which were followed by priests chanting the burial service. No attempt was made to individualize the remains.

The Catacombs are easily reached by taking the Métro to Denfert-Rochereau; you will emerge at the Catacomb's entrance. The cemetery is always open on the first and third Saturdays of the month between 2:00 and 4:00 P.M., with other weekend hours added during the summer. There is a small admission charge, but once inside you're on your own.

Opposite: Entrance to Ossuary
Photo by Louchet; courtesy Direction du Tourisme

After reaching the bottom and walking through initially empty passages, it is startling to come upon what appear to be several miniature cities carved in sandstone and dramatically lit. These sculptures were made by one of the quarry maintenance workers between 1777 and 1782, a M. Decure who, as a soldier of Louis XV, had been held prisoner for several years in the Anglo-Spanish fort of Port Mahon (which he reproduced here). While attempting to construct a staircase for its viewing in 1782, he caused a cave-in and died of his injuries shortly afterward.

The actual entrance to the Ossuary is heralded by several decorated pillars. On the lintel above them is carved, "Stop! This is the Kingdom of the Dead." What follows are walls of packed-together bones, each with a plaque explaining which churchyard that collection came from. While a few have been artistically arranged—one wall has a striking pattern of skulls forming a cross, another of what appears to be an arched church window—most are simply rows of femur knobs, interspersed with an occasional row of skulls.

There is also a pool of water in the middle of the floor that appears somewhat ominous, but it is only a clear spring, used as a reservoir by the Catacombs workers who discovered it. It is best known as The Samaritan Woman's Spring, a reference to the biblical story of Jesus talking with the woman at the well.

One last surprise: a circular security column in the center of the floor decorated completely around with skulls, which caused the little girl just ahead of us to cry out, "Oh la-la, Maman!"

There are many illustrious people buried here, but to separate out their remains from the communal bones of five or six million others would be impossible. **Mirabeau** is here, the popular, if personally unsavory, leader of the Revolution who was first buried in the Panthéon and then ejected. So is the great sixteenth-century comic writer **Rabelais** and **Madeleine Bejart** (Molière's mother-in-law), refugees from the Saint-Paul Saint-Louis churchyard which no longer exists. Victims of the first street fights of the Revolution were brought here, as well as some of those who were subsequently guillotined.

A visit to the Catacombs is really more poignant than depressing. Yet you climb the last stone steps, glad to get back into the sunlight for just a little longer.

Photo by Louchet; courtesy Direction du Tourisme

CHAPTER 13

MONTPARNASSE

▲ ▲ ▲

Death is an angel whose
magnetic palms
Bring dreams of ecstasy and
slumberous calms
To smooth the beds of poor and
naked men.

—BAUDELAIRE

ONE OF THE first things you will see when you enter Montparnasse Cemetery is the amazing four-poster bed of M. and Mme Pigeon. The inventor, Charles, is raised up on one elbow as if a Pigeon lamp has gone off in his head, though his wife sleeps on obliviously (see page 182). Both, however, are dressed in street clothes as is Honoré Champion who sits on the other side of the cemetery in a re-creation of his study. Most of the other inhabitants here have left their furniture at home, but the cemetery has the slightly whimsical feeling that you might expect from one set in an artistic community.

Montparnasse, so the story goes, got its name from a corruption of Mount Parnassos, the legendary home of Apollo, Dionysis, and the Muses. In the beginning there was also a joke attached: the "Mount" referred to a pile of sand and weeds used by students for everything except studying. But a group of notable poets, which included Verlaine, Sully-Prudhomme, and Anatole France, called themselves The Parnassians. A little later Modigliani and Rodin came to Montparnasse because rents were so cheap. Gradually the area developed an artistic sheen and, in time, some of its glamour rubbed off on Montparnasse Cemetery.

Known as *Cimetière du Sud* (Cemetery of the South)

Opposite: Tomb of Gustave Jundt

when it was created from three farms in 1824, Montparnasse comprises 45 acres and 30 sections. The best way to explore it is to take the Métro to Raspail stop, then turn the corner onto Edgar Quinet Boulevard. The first street you come to, Rue Emile Richard, divides the cemetery into an old section and a new section. Some of the division numbers have been used in both sections, but we have designated them as "old" or "new" in our descriptions.

The old cemetery, in which the Pigeons can be found, is to your right as you come down Rue Emile Richard and is a good starting point. It also contains the graves of Guy de Maupassant, César Franck and Colonel Alfred Dreyfus as well as a Brancusi sculpture. When you are finished, retrace your steps back out, and cross the street into the new cemetery. Here lie Jean-Paul Sartre, Jean Seberg, Camille Saint-Saëns, Charles Baudelaire, and several others of note.

DIVISION 2

In this section are two men who resisted the system in different ways. **Pierre-Joseph Proudhon** (1809–1865), a socialist regarded by historians as the Father of Anarchism, whose first book posed the question *What Is Property?* (1840) and answered it, "Property is theft!" He was in prison from 1849 to 1852 for writing critically about Louis Napoléon, then exiled himself to Belgium in 1858 to avoid another jail term for writing *Justice in the Revolution and the Church*. Pardoned in 1862, he returned to Paris to die.

Archeologist **Alexandre Lenoir** (d.1839) who, by creating the Museum of French Monuments, managed to save much of the statuary of St. Denis during the Revolution and still preserve his own life.

DIVISION 3

The most important thing about **Honoré Champion**, an otherwise anonymous scholar, is his tomb by sculptor Albert Bartholmé. Champion is shown seated at his desk in front of curtains and shelves of books.

DIVISION 4

Clara Haskil (1895–1960), Romanian pianist, in a plain tomb with her daughters. Haskil won first prize at the Paris Conservatoire at the age of 14 and went on to concertize with Casals and Enesco. Her Mozart and Schubert recordings are especially valued for their strength and sensitivity.

DIVISION 7

Sculptor **Henri Laurens** (1885–1954), whose tomb shows one of the massive, bulbous figures which were his trademark. This one, *Douleur* (Grief), is prostrate in an attitude of mourning.

DIVISION 8

Tristan Tzara (1896–1963), a Romanian who studied in Zurich, then gravitated to Paris. Tzara was one of the founders of dadaism, a literary and artistic protest movement whose name, meaning horse or hobbyhorse (i.e. favorite idea), he chose at random from a French dictionary. Tzara read the phone book as "poetry" to the accompaniment of cowbells and wrote some works of his own including *The Vaseline Symphony*. Dadaism expanded to the visual arts with works by Hans Arp, Man Ray, and Marcel Duchamp, who gave the Mona Lisa a moustache and goatee. The movement rocked to a halt around 1922.

DIVISION 10

Painter **Henri Fantin-Latour** (1836–1904), best known for his floral studies. Though he considered himself an impressionist and painted *Homage to Delacroix* which showed a number of anti-establishment figures including Manet, Baudelaire, Whistler, and Fantin-Latour himself, he always managed to stay conventional enough to exhibit at the Salon.

DIVISION 11

Urbain Jean Joseph le Verrier (1811–1877), the astronomer who discovered the planet Neptune in 1846.

DIVISION 13

Vincent d'Indy (1851–1931), French composer. A child prodigy, d'Indy began his studies with César Franck in his early twenties and became Franck's chief disciple, virtually deifying him in the process. This extreme view was typical of d'Indy's opinions. In 1894 he established the Schola Cantorum which used Bach and Beethoven as its models; but his catholic interests extended back to Gregorian chants, and his editions and performances of Gluck, Rameau, and Monteverdi did much to aid their revival.

In later years d'Indy became increasingly conservative, opposing the music of Debussy, Ravel, Stravinsky, Prokofiev, and Schoenberg. This was in odd contrast to the encouragement he gave to pupils such as Varese and Roussel. Of his own works, his *Symphony on a French Mountain Air* is still programmed, but other works are seldom heard—though some, such as the *Istar Variations* may deserve revival.

In a mausoleum set farther back from the road is a more famous composer:

CAMILLE SAINT-SAËNS b. *October 9, 1835, Paris; d. December 16, 1921, Algiers.* Caricaturists loved to portray Saint-Saëns as a parrot, picking up on his short-legged strut, beaky nose, and birdlike lisp. Here on the family mausoleum his is just another name, even though he was in the public eye from early childhood. It seems a subdued memorial for such an eccentric and talented life.

Camille was a musical prodigy, much like the Quiz Kids of the postwar radio show. He had perfect pitch and composed his first piano piece at three. Several years later he

---

Ⓐ Charles Pigeon
Ⓑ Gustave Jundt
Ⓒ André Citroën
Ⓓ Frédéric Bartholdi
Ⓔ Alfred Dreyfus
Ⓕ César Franck
Ⓖ Guy de Maupassant
Ⓗ Constantin Brancusi
Ⓘ Camille Saint-Saëns

Ⓙ Vincent d'Indy
   Jean Seberg
Ⓚ Jean-Paul Sartre
Ⓜ Chaim Soutine
Ⓝ Dumont d'Urville
Ⓟ Pierre Laval
Ⓠ Honoré Champion
Ⓡ Charles Baudelaire

MONTPARNASSE

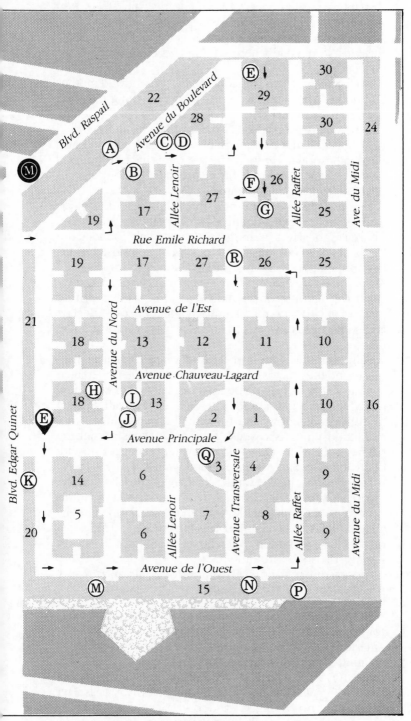

173

was appearing in concert, offering to play any Beethoven sonata for an encore. He was also gifted in philosophy, astronomy, and archeology, often going out to the stone quarries at Meudac where he chipped out fossils for his collection.

Saint-Saëns' genius was coddled by his widowed mother and doting great-aunt, who provided everything the child needed for optimal development. They created a refuge which he never considered leaving. When his mother died he thought of suicide, though he was already 53 and internationally known. He spent the rest of his life traveling and giving concerts, with only his manservant, Gabriel, and his pet dogs to keep him company.

In music there was nothing that Camille could not do well. He held the prestigious post of organist at Madeleine Church for nearly 20 years, gave piano recitals, founded the National Society of Music and, of course, composed. He is best remembered for his *Danse Macabre, Sampson and Delilah,* the *Organ Symphony,* several concertos and, ironically, *The Carnival of the Animals. Carnival* was a private joke parodying Rossini, Offenbach, Mendelssohn, Berlioz and some of his own work and was written in just a few days.

Saint-Saëns was most successful when he stayed with music and the role of boy wonder. A marriage undertaken at 40 to a girl half his age ended dismally. There was real tragedy—his two-year-old son died after a fall from a fourth-story window, and his other son succumbed to a childhood illness six weeks later. Saint-Saëns put all the blame on his wife. On vacation several years later he suddenly left her. She never saw him again.

Left to himself, he wandered through Russia, Greece, Algeria, Spain, England, and America and tried to plan his concert tours to coincide with the natural phenomena which still fascinated him, such as the eruption of Mt. Aetna or an eclipse of the sun. When he died at 86, he was exploring Algeria one more time.

Close to the road, in a very simple tomb, lies an actress of particular interest to Americans.

JEAN SEBERG *b. November 13, 1938, Marshalltown, Iowa; d. August 30, 1979, Paris.* Jean Seberg lived the classic American childhood as immortalized in Norman Rockwell paintings. There were cake sales and Sunday school pageants, hot chocolate and sledding on snowy nights, the smells of chalk dust and new Buster Brown oxfords. Her father, the town druggist, tried to impart to his family the traditional values of achievement and belief in God. Yet

Jean always felt uneasy in this setting. Though she starred in the school plays, her luminous beauty—the wide hazel eyes and cropped light hair that were to become her trademark—was rarely remarked on. She was later to claim that she had never felt appreciated in her hometown.

Jean had just graduated from high school when Otto Preminger began his search for an unknown to play Joan of Arc. Out of eighteen thousand applicants she was selected because of her fresh loveliness. It was soon apparent, however, that at 17 Jean did not have the necessary emotional depth or acting experience. The more Preminger tried to bully it out of her, the stiffer she became. The movie was a disaster, a particular target of critics who were weary of Preminger's constant hype.

Such wholesale panning was an ego-crushing experience for the young teenager. Though she stuck with acting and in time developed respectable skills to go with her beauty, Jean never really trusted herself again. She made 37 films, among them *Breathless, The Mouse That Roared, Paint Your Wagon* and *Lilith*, but drifted into bad movies just as easily, accepting scripts that degraded her.

If Jean had never left Marshalltown, chances are that she would not have married three times, gotten mixed up with the Black Panthers, or ended up hospitalized as insane. Her most famous husband was her second: writer and diplomat Romain Gary, 24 years older than she. Partly to wean him from his wife, Jean had become pregnant and given birth to their son, Diego, in July, 1962. She and Romain formally separated six years after their marriage.

By then Jean had little sense of reality left. She (and her pocketbook) were easy prey for Black Panther leader, Hakim Jamal. Although her humanitarian instincts were sound, much of her emotion and cash went directly to Jamal, a charismatic con artist with whom she began a passionate affair. He caught her up in his persecution fantasies, convincing her that he had narrowly escaped assassination time after time and that she was under surveillance. Ironically, in her case it almost became true. The FBI, alarmed by her involvement in the Black Power movement, kept a dossier on Seberg and did what they could to discredit her publicly.

The cruelest example of this discrediting was the "leaking" of a number of gossip column items suggesting that the baby she was pregnant with was interracial. It wasn't. But Nina Hart Gary, born prematurely to an overwrought mother in August, 1970, only lived for two days. Jean was inconsolable. Perhaps the baby had represented her last chance for something worthwhile, and when that was gone she felt she had nothing. She thrashed around, grasping at liquor, casual affairs, anything that might deaden the feeling of irrevocable loss.

Nothing did. In the last year of her life she was hospitalized several times and became involved with a 19-year-old Algerian. It was he who finally alerted the police to what he called her "disappearance."

Jean was found 10 days later on the back seat of her car under a blanket, an empty barbituate bottle and a note to her son in her hand. In it she begged his forgiveness and told him to be strong. Yet the police were troubled by several discrepancies. Jean would have had to drive to the place where the car was found but would never have done so without her glasses—which were back in her apartment. Several additional inconsistencies gave police the impression that someone may have watched her die. But nothing was ever proved, and the case was closed.

DIVISION 15

In this section is a decorated stele to **Jules Sebastien Dumont d'Urville** (1790–1842), an admiral who sailed twice around the world, discovered and purchased such works of art as the *Vénus de Milo* and also explored Antarctica. His wife and young son are buried here with him, all victims of a fire in their coach in 1842.

Pierre Laval (1883–1945), lies here with his wife in a quiet tomb which belies his turbulent end. As French premier and foreign minister during World War II, he advocated collaboration with the Germans and instituted his own reign of terror. After the war he was tried and, despite protestations of patriotism, was convicted of treason. He made an unsuccessful suicide attempt but was executed after having his stomach pumped.

Finally, in a grave that would no doubt have made him as unhappy as everything else did, painter:

CHAIM SOUTINE *b. 1893, Smilovitchi, Belorussia; d. August 9, 1943, Paris.* Chaim Soutine was the quintessence of the tortured artist, a tormented soul who expected to come to a bad end. In this he was not disappointed. When he died at 49 of a perforated ulcer, it was because, being Jewish, he had fled to the countryside during World War II and was unable to return to Paris quickly enough for an operation.

Chaim, a sensitive and brooding shoe mender's son, got into art school at Vilna, Russia, at 17 by weeping and imploring the director to take him (he had failed the entrance exam). From there he went to Paris in 1911 and studied at the Ecole des Beaux-Arts—though its classical influence is difficult to see in his work. His unique style was there from the beginning: faces resembling the bulbous-nosed rubber masks that adults buy for Halloween, sides of decomposing beef, wildly writhing trees which seem possessed of evil spirits.

In Paris Chaim survived by living in a collection of ramshackle buildings left over from the Paris Exposition of 1900. It was there that he met Modigliani (whom he later blamed for making him an alcoholic) and Chagall, who quickly learned to turn wet canvases to the wall to avoid their being brushed by Soutine's filthy overcoat. His poverty was hardly romantic; Chaim made clothes from parts of other apparel and would sometimes stand for hours at a café counter, hoping someone would offer to buy him coffee or a sandwich.

Yet when his paintings became popular in 1922 and were bought by museums as examples of expressionism, he was hardly any happier. He still destroyed canvases which displeased him, and, though he had had a daughter by his young mistress Deborah Melnik in 1925, he refused to recognize her as his child. Soutine lived with several women during his lifetime, but none of them were able to calm his troubled spirit.

His grave is a bad joke. Though he did not always observe the taboos he was raised with as an Orthodox Jew, neither did he turn his back on his heritage; yet here he is, spending eternity under the weight of a long marble cross, placed here by his last mistress, Marie Berthe Aurenche. It is probably no worse than what he expected.

DIVISION 17 (new cemetery)

Charles Augustin Sainte-Beuve (1804–1869), brilliant critic and writer who consoled himself for his imagined ugliness with Adele Hugo, Victor's wife. His motto was "Truth and truth alone. And let the good and the beautiful look after themselves as best they can." Yet one wonders whether his scowling, double-chinned monument by José de Charmoy, though set strikingly on a huge, high pillar, might contain less beauty and more truth than even he would have liked.

DIVISION 17 (old cemetery)

Painter **Gustave Jundt** (1830–1884), whose palette is being decorated with flowers by a pigtailed child in Alsatian dress, looks out over the cemetery with an expression of zest. Born in Strasbourg, Jundt specialized in sentimental illustrations of children.

DIVISION 18

Constantin Brancusi (1876–1957), a sculptor whose work in wood and stone was so simple that he himself referred to it as "sculpture for the blind." He left Romania at 11 to see the world and eventually came to Paris, where he remained for the next 50 years, living only with a white spitz, Polaris. One of his sculptures, *Le Baiser*, is in Division 19 (see photo below).

DIVISION 20

Here, in the plainest of graves and across the street from the place he lived all his adult life, is one of France's best-loved philosophers.

JEAN-PAUL SARTRE *b. June 21, 1905, Paris; d. April 15, 1980, Paris.* The setting is a slightly delapidated sitting room in the 1940s. The characters are three unhappy people and one cheerful proprietor (the Devil). The action? Nothing to speak of.

Opposite: Charles Augustin Sainte-Beuve

Jean-Paul Sartre's play *No Exit* presents hell as an endless repetition of days spent in the same place with the same people and no chance of creating a future that will be any different. In his last years, almost blind and writing very little, Sartre complained to his lifetime companion, Simone de Beauvoir, "I have the feeling of perpetually living the same day over again. I see you, I see Arlette, various doctors . . . and then it is all repeated." To Sartre, being unable to carve out new territory was almost the same as being dead.

Yet not quite. His philosophy of existentialism was based on the tenet that man is not predisposed by his nature to any particular behavior or thinking (even in old age) but must create himself anew through daily choices. This thesis, which he expounded in *Being and Nothingness* and *Criticism of Dialectical Reason* earned him a permanent place among philosophers.

Sartre strove to practice what he preached in his own life. At one point he aligned himself with Communism, yet later condemned the Soviet invasion of Afghanistan and supported the American boycott of the 1980 Olympics. He was always sympathetic to the left, however, and despite the fluctuations in his fortunes, always lived in the same modest apartment on Boulevard Raspail, overlooking Montparnasse Cemetery.

In this neighborhood were his friends, his favorite cafés (including Café Raspail Vert, where he lingered over coffee and the news), and the ambiance that allowed him to pursue new adventures while not worrying about material details. So committed was he to his right of endless self-re-creation that he refused the Nobel Prize in 1964, commenting that it would turn him into "an institution." He also refused the French equivalent of knighthood, the Legion of Honor, though his countrymen attempted unsuccessfully to force it on him.

In childhood, Sartre had been the epitome of the skinny little kid with thick glasses and all the answers. When he was an infant his father died, and he was raised in his maternal grandfather's home. His grandfather, an uncle of Albert Schweitzer and founder of France's Modern Language Institute, fostered the child's precocity and his ability to reason.

Jean-Paul also had an early certainty of his own ugliness. Walleyed and physically puny, he did not let his looks interfere with his romantic conquests. These were plentiful and remained so throughout his lifetime, though no relationship compared with the one he had with Simone de Beauvoir. Both were philosophically opposed to marriage. They lived in nearby apartments, always traveled together, and saw each other daily as they pursued parallel courses.

True to his need for diverse experiences, Sartre served in the French army, taught in Le Havre and Berlin as well as in Paris, was incarcerated as a prisoner of war during World War II, and was arrested in 1970 for left-wing protest activities. Though he remained charming, vibrant, intense, and sometimes melancholy, he gradually released his hold on life. As his sight waned, he increasingly felt his work was done.

Yet his death from kidney failure at 74 was a shock to those around him. Fifty thousand people followed the hearse to Montparnasse to pay tribute to the author of *Being and Nothingness, The Age of Reason, Nausea, The Flies, No Exit,* and over 40 other works. Most bereaved of all was Simone de Beauvoir. In her memoir *Adieux* she tells of the verbal games they played as students at the University of Paris and how, when one scored a brilliant victory over the other, the winner would tease, "There you are in your little box!"

In bidding him farewell, de Beauvoir wrote, "You are in your little box; you will not come out of it and I will not join you there. Even if I am buried next to you there will be no communication between your ashes and mine." Yet in looking back over what turned out to be her closest relationship and one that lasted over 50 years, she felt compelled to add, "That is how things are. It is in itself splendid that we were able to live out our lives in harmony for so long."

DIVISION 21

General **Gaston de Galiffet** (1830–1909), who was on the wrong side of both the Paris Commune and the Dreyfus Affair.

DIVISION 22

Charles Pigeon, inventor of an inexplosible gas lamp, which gained wide popularity before electricity replaced it. He is shown, as mentioned, with his wife in their famous double bed.

DIVISION 25

Nicolas Conté (1755–1805) who, on Napoléon's Egyptian expedition, invented the pencil by melting down bullets and putting the lead into reeds from the Nile (after he and his companions had exhausted their own implements copying down hieroglyphics). He went on to manufacture the Conté crayon.

DIVISION 26 (old cemetery)

In a substantial coffin with his bronzed visage on the end is **César Franck** (1822–1890). Franck, the Belgian-born composer, was a child prodigy whose pianistic talents were exploited by his father. His family moved to Paris when he was 15, and a year later he took first prize in piano, going so far as to show off in the Conservatory finals by transposing a difficult piece into another key at first sight. He secured a first prize in counterpoint two years later, but after that his career slowed down dramatically. He became an organ virtuoso and his *Six Pièces pour Grand Orgue* (1862) are all that are played of his early works.

Strongly influenced by Wagner, he developed a loyal following of students including Duparc, Chausson, d'Indy and Pierné. His great popularity has waned in the last 50 years. His *D Minor Symphony* remains his most popular work; his *Quartet in D*, the *Piano Quartet*, and the *Prelude Chorale and Fugue* are all still played, but by and large his voluptuous chromaticism is a style not appreciated in our time.

The other noted occupant of this section is author:

GUY DE MAUPASSANT *b. August 5, 1850, Sotteville; d. July 6, 1893, Paris.* Guy de Maupassant stands out as an oddly contemporary figure: He was a civil servant who hated his job and wanted to be a full-time writer; he got caught up in living on credit beyond his means; and, though he often wrote pornography, he was nevertheless devoted to sailing and outdoor living. Today he would have sold stories for large amounts to *Esquire* and *Playboy* and probably have made a movie sale or two.

A large, hearty-looking man with a bristly black moustache, Guy's looks belied the health problems which would kill him at 42. His mother, a childhood friend of Gustave Flaubert, encouraged her son's literary ambitions and wrote Flaubert letters beseeching him to help Guy. But though Flaubert did befriend him (his other mentor was poet Louis Boilhet), the younger man would probably have succeeded on his own.

Maupassant began by publishing psychological horror stories and gradually developed other themes: family quarrels and greed, ambition and suicide, deviance in sexual behavior—subjects which titillated his respectable audience, yet gave him scope to satirize that audience as well.

Most Americans are familiar with Maupassant through his two most anthologized stories: "The Necklace," which tells of a young woman who borrows jewelry from a rich friend, loses it, and spends the rest of her life paying for its replacement, only to find out in the end that it was paste; and "A Piece of String," a tale about a miser who is ashamed to admit that all he picked up from the ground was a bit of string and is condemned to death for an imagined theft.

Once Maupassant's work gained popularity, he was able to quit his job at the Ministry of Education and the Arts and write full-time. He bought a new yacht which he kept moored along the Côte d'Azur, renovated his apartment,

and built a country home in Etretat—all the while supporting his mother, his brother (who later became insane), and
eventually his brother's family. Guy himself never married,
preferring a circle of congenial friends and the life of a
bachelor.

Yet like a character in one of his stories whose life is not
what it seems, his success was a facade being eaten from
beneath. He suffered from bouts of blindness and neuralgia
(the result of an early bout of tertiary syphilis), which left
him in constant pain. He dared not stop writing long
enough to try and recover—his lifestyle kept him constantly in debt. Eventually he had no choice. He spent the last
year of his life plagued by madness and confined to an
asylum.

The irony which he so richly portrayed in his work pursued him into the grave. In his will Maupassant had asked to

be buried without a coffin, so that his remains might better mingle with the nature he loved; instead, he was interred in a triple box of oak, pine, and zinc. A confirmed skeptic, he was given a religious burial. And, though he had not been estranged from them, his parents did not attend. Perhaps he would at least have liked his bier, a railed-in planting of shrubs with an open book above them.

DIVISION 27 (new cemetery)

The cenotaph of Charles Pierre Baudelaire by José de Charmoy (who also created the stele of Saint-Beuve) is closer to the spirit of the poet than the family plot in Division 6. On Charmoy's memorial the poet broods over a gauze-encased body lying beneath him.

CHARLES PIERRE BAUDELAIRE *b. April 9, 1821, Paris; d. August 31, 1867, Paris.* In the year before his death Baudelaire, resting in a nursing home and left all but mute from advanced syphilis, nevertheless enjoyed some respite from his deepening depression. He took special pleasure in his many visitors, in Berthe Morisot's playing Wagner on the piano, and in the numerous flowers which grew in the yard outside the home. His condition also allowed his mother, Caroline, one last chance to play a maternal role and thereby attempt a long overdue reconciliation. But to the dying man unable to speak, such a reconciliation was difficult.

As a child, Baudelaire was deeply attached to his mother. This closeness undoubtedly increased after the death of his father when the boy was five. However, when Caroline married Captain Jacques Aupick a year and a half later, Charles was forced to compete for her affections with a successful soldier, a man who would rise to become a general and a diplomat, and a man who exhibited all the pomp and importance of his posts. Young Charles lost the battle.

This rejection was heightened by his mother's constant criticisms of his efforts. Fearing compliments would spoil him, she praised him only to others. As her attitude became habitual, his resentment became ingrained. Both became permanent characteristics of their relationship.

Baudelaire's behavior as a young man quickly brought his relationship with his stepfather into eclipse. He worked little, spent freely to support the tastes of a dandy, and contracted gonorrhea and syphilis. Finally he took up with Jeanne Duval, a poorly educated, bit-part actress, the daughter of an interracial prostitute. Supporting her increased his debt and forced his mother to have his inheritance placed in trust. He chafed under this humiliation for the rest of his life.

His liaison with Jeanne hardly served to compensate. She inspired him with her beauty but, moody, lethargic, and ill-read, she had little else to offer. The relationship turned neurotic and occasionally violent. All of this is apparent in the many love poems he wrote about Jeanne. They often parted and were often reunited. Baudelaire had two other love affairs, both short-lived. With age he became increasingly misogynous.

Oddly, Baudelaire retained a strong, if limited, sense of conventional morality and came to abjure sex and hashish. He was, however, a habitual user of alcohol and of opium, which he took in the form of laudinum. These in combination with his syphilis became the trinity of his demise.

Baudelaire is known for his art criticism and for his translations of Poe and DeQuincey, but his fame lies chiefly with his book, *Les Fleurs du Mal*. In their time these poems were shocking for their subject matter, their frankness, and their neurotic and cynical melancholy. Indeed, a trial was held, and six of the poems were removed by censors for being "obscene." The book's critical reception was mixed, and it was only after the poet's death that his fame and influence were felt.

According to his mother, Baudelaire died with a smile on his lips. Whether this signified reconciliation or release one can only guess. Perhaps one clue is the monument at the family grave which honors Général and Mme Aupick, but indicates only the presence of Charles. His worth as a poet is not acknowledged.

DIVISION 28

Frédéric Auguste Bartholdi (1834–1904), best known to Americans for the Statue of Liberty. Bartholdi studied architecture in his native Alsace, but on a trip to Egypt and the pyramids his taste for large scale sculpture was whetted. Besides *Liberty Enlightening the World* (1886), he also created the huge *Lion of Belfort* (1880) in Belfort, France, and the statue on Gustav Jundt's tomb (Division 17).

In a plain mausoleum not shaped like an automobile rests:

ANDRÉ CITROËN *b. February 5, 1879, Paris; d. July 3, 1935, Paris.* Known as the Henry Ford of France, André Citroën shared many of the characteristics of his American counterpart. Born of penniless Dutch parents, André made his first fortune supplying French ammunition for World War I. During that time he also introduced floodlighting to

Charles Pierre Baudelaire cenotaph

Paris and reorganized the city's postal system and autobus service. After the war, continuing to operate as if he were running a small town instead of one of the world's largest cities, he turned his munitions factories into automobile-making plants.

Everything Citroën did was on a large scale: employing over thirty thousand men in 10 factories, backing African trade route expeditions, and gambling in a way that struck terror to his wife's heart. (On one historic evening he calmly lost $400,000 at a single sitting, while she wept and pleaded with him to stop.) A huge sign on the Eiffel Tower flashed out his name, then showed a barometer with the temperature, which gave way to a clock with the time.

Unable to scale down, even in the face of the Depression and a field of new competitors, Citroën saw his company fall into bankruptcy. He died of cancer a few months after losing control to his largest creditor, the Michelin Tire Company.

DIVISION 29

Charles Cros (1842–1888) who designed the phonograph (on paper) before Edison, experimented with new techniques in color photography, and tried to contact life on other planets.

Finally, in a monument so plain you might easily overlook it, is Alfred Dreyfus, unwitting eye of a storm that rocked Europe.

The Separation of a Couple *by de Max*

ALFRED DREYFUS *b. October 9, 1859, Mulhouse, Alsace; d. July 12, 1935, Paris.* Nearly one hundred years later, the Dreyfus Affair still rankles.

Part of the problem lies in the personality of Alfred Dreyfus himself. A rather colorless individual without great breadth or humor, had he not been in the wrong place in the wrong decade, he would have moved through history unnoticed. Dreyfus lived for his wife and two children and for his military career, which he had achieved through intelligence and obedience to military discipline. The only difference between him and other staff officers was that he

Tomb of Julio Ruelas, an unknown, Division 26

happened to be Jewish.

It is Dreyfus's dedication and good faith that make what happened continue to be painful, that allow the Army no extenuating circumstances. When a list of secret French documents was found in the wastebasket of the German embassy in Paris, Dreyfus was arbitrarily accused of being a spy. And though handwriting experts testified at the trial that the writing was not his, a secret message from the Minister of War ordered the court martial judges to find him guilty.

Captain Dreyfus was imprisoned on Devil's Island (off French Guiana) in 1894. But his case would not die. Another staff officer, Georges Picquart, located a more likely culprit, a Major Charles Esterhazy, and found proof. This proof was suppressed "for the good of the Army" for as long as possible, but finally, amid public outcry, Esterhazy was tried—and acquitted within minutes. It next came out that further corroborating evidence against Dreyfus had been forged by another officer, a Major Henry. Henry committed suicide, Esterhazy fled to England, and the public demanded a new trial.

The notoriety of the case might have died there, had not the military court—unable to ever admit a mistake—reconvicted Dreyfus, albeit with "extenuating circumstances"! This time the outcry was heard round the world. In an attempt to save face, the Army offered Dreyfus a pardon which, to the disappointment of his enthusiastic supporters, he accepted. But in 1906 he was exonerated by the Court of Appeals and decorated with the Legion of Honor. He resumed his army career and the atmosphere which had fostered such blatant anti-Semitism (see Drumont) subsided.

Dreyfus refused to be cast in a heroic role or fight for other "causes." "I was only an artillery officer who, because of a tragic mistake, was prevented from pursuing his career," he insisted. "Dreyfus the symbol of justice—that's not me." Many of his disillusioned supporters would have agreed.

But Dreyfus had already served his time in hell, living through the humiliation of the trials and bearing a continuing legacy from Devil's Island: recurring attacks of malaria, nightmares about his treatment, and an inability, after years of silence, to communicate even with his family.

As a trained soldier, Dreyfus no doubt knew what he was doing in retreating. After his reinstatement, when he had ventured out to attend the transfer of Zola's ashes to the Panthéon in 1908, he was shot in the arm by a fanatical journalist named Gregory. Gregory was captured at the scene, tried—and unanimously acquitted.

CHAPTER 14

LA CHAPELLE EXPIATOIRE

▲ ▲ ▲

The sunlight on the garden
Hardens and grows cold,
We cannot cage the minute
Within its nets of gold,
When all is told
We cannot beg for pardon.

—LOUIS MACNEICE

IN 1792 THE NOBILITY were no more popular dead than alive. Their guillotined corpses were dumped in open rubbish carts and taken to the nearest burial ground—for a long time St. Madeleine parish churchyard. There they were tossed into large trenches and sprinkled with quicklime to hasten their decomposition. No markers were erected. The fate of the royal couple was the same as everyone else's.

In 1797 the property, abandoned as soon as it was saturated, was bought by Olivier Desclozeaux, a wealthy lawyer with Royalist leanings. He lived just across the street and had watched the royal burials from his window, so that when Louis XVIII began his melancholy search for Louis XVI and Marie Antoinette 21 years later, Desclozeaux was able to point out their locations. (He was also able to sell Louis the property for a hefty sum.)

On the spot where the bodies were recovered, Louis XVIII erected an expiatory chapel "to beg pardon for France." He commissioned the architect Pierre Fontaine to design a neoclassical chapel with a crypt and a memorial garden. And though from time to time unrepentant types have wanted to tear down this somber reminder and put up apartments instead, La Chapelle Expiatoire has been protected as a national monument since 1914.

To reach the chapel, take the Métro to the Havre Caumartin stop and turn onto Rue Pasquier. Go to number 29, pay a nominal admission, then go up the stairs and outside.

The first view of the gardens with the chapel looming behind them is unexpectedly moving. Along each side is a row of symbolic stone tombs erected to honor the six hundred soldiers of the Swiss Guard who, when defending the Tuileries Gardens, were inexplicably ordered by Louis XVI not to fire back and were subsequently massacred by the crowd.

But the monuments also represent a number of colorful personalities who were guillotined and buried here. Among them were:

Mme du Barry, former shopgirl and professional beauty, whose last job title was "Mistress to Louis XV." She stayed with him until he died horribly of smallpox, then she was sent to a convent to prevent her telling "state secrets." A year later she was given back her freedom, but she might have been better off confined: she was accused by the Tribunal of "having dissipated the treasure of the state and worn mourning for a tyrant" and, screaming with fright, was dragged off to the scaffold.

Duc d'Orléans (1747–1793), a cousin and rival of the King. He changed his name to Philippe Egalité and voted for the death penalty for Louis XVI—but neither action saved him from the same fate. An epicure, gambler, and heavy drinker, he begged a 24-hour stay of execution so he could enjoy one final repast. He died with a smile on his lips and a succinct obscenity.

Mme Roland (1754–1793), a witty, passionate young woman, wife of the Minister of the Interior, whose salon helped to foment the Revolution. She eventually sickened of the constant bloodshed as one faction turned on another. She herself was condemned to death when the Girondins, her party, fell out of favor. Looking up at the statue in the Place de la Révolution, she uttered her famous epigraph, "Ah, Liberty, what crimes are committed in your name!"

Charlotte Corday (1768–1793). See Marat, pages 106–107.

Jacques René Hébert (1757–1794), publisher of a vituperative and hysterical political rag, *Le Père Duchesne*. Tiny, fastidious, and reeking of musk, he lost several jobs because of embezzlement before finding success as a journalist. Hébert detested Marie Antoinette in particular and screamed for her execution. But he was hoisted with his own petard when his party lost favor, and he was guillotined, fainting and moaning.

General **Armand-Louis Custine** (1793), a marquis who was dismissed of his command and condemned before the Tribunal for pitying Louis XVI, forbidding the circulation of *Le Père Duchesne* among his soldiers, and "eating with aristocrats instead of good republicans."

Jacques Pierre Brissot (1754–1793), lawyer, and then editor of the *Patriote Français*, who traveled to Philadelphia and returned home impressed by the Quakers. In that frame of mind he argued for sparing the King's life. Unsuccessful, he lost his own as well, dying with the words, *Vive la République!* on his lips.

Despite their very diverse political and social views, all met the same fate, bringing to mind Mme Roland's other comment, "The time has come which was foretold, when the people would ask for bread and be given corpses."

La Chapelle Expiatoire, impressive from without, is tiny inside. Two statues dominate its interior, that of Marie Antoinette on the left and Louis XVI on the right. The Queen is shown being upheld by "Religion"—actually her sister-in-law, Elizabeth—to whom she was very close. On the base of the monument is the text of the moving letter Marie Antoinette wrote to Elizabeth on the eve of her execution, begging her help in caring for her children. Elizabeth died before she could read it, but it was discovered in the Queen's cell and preserved. Louis XVI's statue shows him on his knees being instructed by an angel.

Downstairs, the crypt is grey-white and silent, with a stone tile floor. In an alcove is a black marble coffin, surrounded by porcelain wreaths and faded streamers, belated funerary remembrances from other branches of the royal family. Although the physical remains of Louis XVI and Marie Antoinette were moved back to the safety of St. Denis, it is here in this quiet and empty place that the spirit of the unfortunate King and Queen are really felt.

MARIE ANTOINETTE *b. November 2, 1755, Vienna; d. October 16, 1793, Paris.* **LOUIS XVI** *b. 1754, Paris; d. January 21, 1793, Paris.*

> Meanwhile, the fair young Queen in
> her halls of state. . .heeds not the
> future; least of all dreads it. Fair young
> daughter of Time, what things time has
> in store for thee!
> Thomas Carlyle, *The French Revolution*

Marie Antoinette and Louis XVI are like figures glimpsed through a far-off castle window. They waltz in a rectangle of yellow light and we can almost see their faces—but not their hearts. Did that sharp-featured, heavily bejeweled woman destroy her family through her extravagance and pride, or was she merely caught in history's cruel machine? Was that corpulent, faintly smiling man good-hearted and generous, or merely a glutton and a blunderer?

After the Revolution, historians still felt compelled to take sides and left no objective picture of what the King and Queen were actually like. The facts are these: Princess Maria Antonia of Austria was a giddy 15-year-old when she was sent to France with 50 carriages of her belongings to wed the young Louis and help cement Franco-Austrian relations. Except for learning Italian, she had spent her time at play. Louis, for his part, was stammering and obese, a 15-year-old who enjoyed hunting, locksmithing, and eating.

It was not an inspired union. The young princess soon learned to take her pleasures in plays and operas, close female friends, and, eventually, a young Swede named Axel von Fersen. Louis continued to hunt and to eat till he passed out. Then, prematurely, the death of Louis XV from smallpox forced the 20-year-old couple onto the throne. They wept that they were "too young" to reign but took their place in the royal line.

The young King was well-liked, a regard that never entirely diminished, but his Queen pleased no one. Her extravagance in decorating, entertaining, and buying jewelry was criticized, and she alienated the nobility by conferring favors and pensions on her favorites. Things calmed down temporarily in 1877 when, after seven years, Louis consummated the marriage and gave the masses a baby princess to adore. (Realizing her pregnancy, Marie Antoinette had approached Louis with a "complaint": "Sire, one of your subjects has kicked me in the stomach!" The King was ecstatic.)

They became excellent parents and dutiful monarchs, but the times were against them. If the country had not been so near bankruptcy that occasionally there was not even enough flour to make bread, if taxation among the three classes had not been so skewed, and if the nobility had not been pushing for a political system in which the upper classes would rule, it might have been possible for the King and Queen to have been merely exiled instead of murdered.

But the masses, who began by demanding bread, were soon hungry for blood. And the royal pair ignored the signs. Louis wavered when he should have stood firm, gave lip service to the Revolution while secretly negotiating with other rulers to quash it. And, like a person trying to rescue belongings during a fire and getting burned to death instead, Marie Antoinette focused on trying to save the monarchy for her sons.

When they did finally see that they were in mortal danger, they tried to escape. Their disguised carriage almost made it to the German border before they were captured and marched back to Paris in disgrace. This time the iron gates clanged shut. Their appeals to her family and to other crowned heads of Europe brought no effective help. Her parents were dead and her brother didn't care.

Louis XVI was tried and guillotined on January 21, 1793, proclaiming, "Frenchmen, I am innocent." Marie Antoinette was charged with treasonous activities a few months later and, in a shameful attempt to make the prosecution's case stronger, was accused of sexual activities with eight-year-old Louis XVII. (The unhappy child was to die two years later of the bone-softening hereditary tuberculosis which had claimed his older brother.) On October 16, 1793, still terrified for her children's fate, Marie Antoinette was brought to the scaffold on an open rubbish cart.

C H A P T E R   1 5

ST. DENIS

▲ ▲ ▲

*The monuments of noble men
are their virtues.*

—EURIPIDES

AT FIRST GLANCE, the royal tombs at St. Denis seem a bewildering collection of marble sunbathers. You may be tempted to wander past the reclining bodies quickly, stopping to look at only the most unusual. To do so would be to miss a unique dimension of French history, a whole pantheon of virtuous and less-than-virtuous personalities. If the French Revolution had never occurred, there would be even more tombs to see.

When the Convention passed a resolution to "demolish those mausoleums which recall the terrifying memory of our kings," angry sans-culottes descended on St. Denis with sledgehammers. The remains of royalty were unearthed, thrown in a pit, and drenched in quicklime to speed their final disintegration. Gold and silver statues, religious relics (including an alleged bone of Isaiah), and treasures such as Joan of Arc's sword were taken to the Convention to be broken up. Lead coffins were melted down for bullets.

Fortunately archeologist Alexandre Lenoir was given permission to move a number of stone and marble statues to his newly formed Museum of French Monuments where they remained unscathed. With the restoration of the monarchy in 1814, Louis XVIII worked to repair the damage. A new lead roof was put on the basilica, stained-glass windows were returned to their frames, and a number of "restorers" were hired to put the statuary back in place.

The result was comical. A writer of the times, Baron de Guihermy, wrote that "having listed all their characters,

Opposite: Bertrand du Guesclin

they decreed that each marble king would have the right to a wife of the same material to share the boredom of the grave with him . . . Princes of the second order were condemned to handing over their wives, whether they liked it or not." Bewigged heads were added to early crusaders, kings who had never had mausoleums were treated to newly created resting places.

Finally the people rebelled, and in 1859 the talented architect, Eugène Viollet-le-Duc, was called in to make things right. He consulted the historical notations and returned the tombs to their original places (Louis XVIII had consigned half to the crypt), then removed inaccurate and ridiculous restorations. One thing he could not do, of course, was return the violated bones to their correct places; most of them were reburied in the crypt, to await reassemblage at the final trumpet.

St. Denis Basilica is said to have begun with a burial, that of the saint who, after being beheaded, walked here from Montmartre and was buried in a Gallo-Roman cemetery on the site. Early Christians gathered to worship at his grave, which St. Geneviève protected with an abbey in A.D.475. The Abbey of St. Denis was replaced in 630 by King Dagobert and one hundred years later an Abbot Fulrad built a church on the site. Around 1140 another abbot, Suger, replaced it. The narthex and apse which he created still survive, but the current cathedral was erected between 1231 and 1281, using the designs of Pierre de Montreuil.

The second royal burial was that of Aregund (d. ca. 565), second wife of Lothar I. Although St. Germain-des-Prés had been designated the royal burial site, Dagobert also chose St. Denis, as did his son Clovis II. Other kings began to select the basilica for burial, and by A.D. 1200 it was firmly entrenched as the Cemetery of Kings.

To reach St. Denis, take the Métro to the last stop, St. Denis Basilica; the cathedral will be in sight. Enter through the back door and go down on the right to the admission window. There are over 70 monuments, statues, and *gisants* (life-sized sculptures of the deceased on their coffin lids) in the church itself, some more significant than others. We have identified all of them on the map but described only those that seem especially important or that belong to people of particular interest. The numbers correspond to those on the map.

(2) **Louis d'Orléans** (d.1407), who was killed on the streets of Paris by his nephew, John the Fearless, when both were competing for the throne. Louis, from Burgundy, had acted as adviser to his incapacitated brother, Charles the Mad, and wanted the throne himself. But John objected,

setting off a civil war between the Burgundians and the Armagnacs. Louis lies next to his wife, **Valentine de Milan** (d.1408).

(7) This elaborate tomb is that of **François I** (d.1547) and his wife **Claudia** (d.1524). A handsome, chivalrous, and intellectually brilliant young king who originated free study and the College of France, François' early promise dissipated into lechery and self-indulgence. His marriage to Claudia, undertaken to settle the question of Breton independence, did not stop his amorous adventures. In the style of Renaissance tombs, François and Claudia are shown praying with their children on the upper level and naked in the throes of death on the coffin itself.

(11) **Philip III the Bold** (d.1285). His white gisant on black marble smiles beneficently. Despite his name, his reign was uneventful. When he died during a Crusade, his flesh was economically boiled away from his bones in a mixture of wine and water, so that the bones could be sent to St. Denis along with his heart.

(13) **Louis III** (d.882) who, pursuing a woman he found attractive, was thrown from his horse and died.

(14) **Carloman** (d.884), who was speared to death when a servant mistook him for a wild boar.

(16) **Pépin the Short** (d.768), who wanted to be buried on his belly outside the main doors of the church, to atone for the sins of his father **Charles Martel** (#8). Martel had confiscated Church property to raise money for war against the Muslims of Spain and various tribes of Germany.

(19) **Charles V the Wise** (d. 1380). Sculpted during his lifetime by artist André Beauneuveu, his statue portrays a physically frail Charles. Unlike his predecessors he did not crave glory on the battlefield, preferring quiet pursuits such as successfully building up the library of the Louvre.

(20) **Charles VI** (d. 1422), whose short, anxious gisant hints at the madness that plagued him throughout his life. Inheriting the kingdom at 12, he soon collapsed under a frantic pace of pleasure. Though occasionally lucid, he was unfit to rule for his last 30 years, despite the machinations of his wife **Isabel of Bavaria** (d. 1435, # 21).

(22) **Bertrand du Guesclin** (d.1380), a knight from Brittany whom Charles V made the constable of France. It was a rare honor for a commoner's bones to be buried at St. Denis. De Guesclin's heart went to Dinan, his entrails to Puy, and his flesh to Montferrand—popular French centers at the time. In keeping with his status, his gisant is smaller and lower to the floor than the others.

(23) Although they are not buried up here, after climbing the stairs beside the altar you will see statues of Marie

1	Charles, Count of Valois	36	Mary of Bourbon-Vendôme
2	Louis d'Orléans	37	Dagobert
	Valentine Milan	38	Philip VI
3	Béatrice of Bourbon	39	Jean II
4	François I (heart)	40	Philip V the Tall
5	Marguerite of Flanders	41	Jeanne of Evreux
6	François II (heart)	42	Charles IV
7	François I and Claudia	43	Blanche of France
8	Charles Martel	44	Henri II (tomb)
9	Clovis II		Catherine de Médici
10	Isabelle of Aragon	45	Du Chastel
11	Philip III the Bold	46	Hermentrude
12	Philip IV the Good	47	Carloman
13	Louis III	48	Philip, son of Louis VI
14	Carloman	49	Jeanne of France
15	Bertha	50	Constance of Castille
16	Pépin the Short	51	Jean I
17	Louis of Santerre	52	Robert the Pious
18	Jeanne of Bourbon	53	Henri I
19	Charles V the Wise	54	Louis IV
20	Charles VI	55	Constance of Arles
21	Isabel of Bavaria	56	Louis X
22	Bertrand du Guesclin	57	Louis XII and Anne
23	Statues of Louis XVI	58	Louis, Cardinal
	and Marie Antoinette	59	Henri III
24	Léon of Lusignan	60	Philip of France
25	Mary of Spain	61	Louis of France
26	Charles of Valois	62	Charles, King of Sicily
27	unknown princess	63	Renée of Orléans
28	unknown princess	64	Blanche of France
29	Blanche of France	65	Blanche of Evreux
30	Jean of France	66	Jeanne of France
31	Robert of Artois	67	Charles, Count of Valois
32	Childebert	68	unknown queen
33	Clovis I	69	Louis of France
34	Frédegund	70	Marguerite of Artois
35	Henri II (statues)	70	Clémence of Hungary
	Catherine de Médici		

ST. DENIS

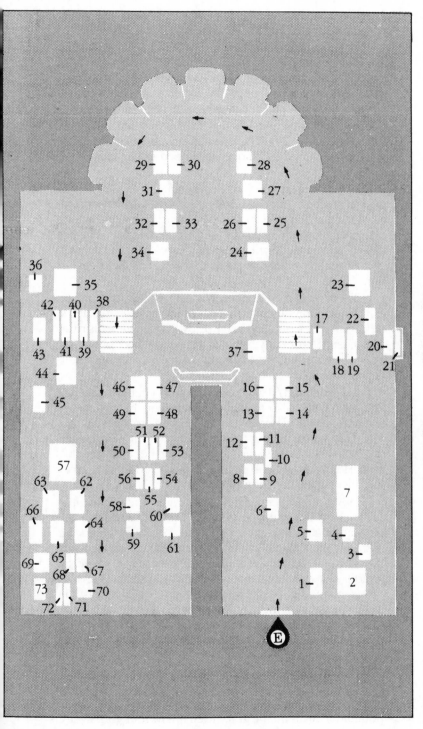

Antoinette and Louis XVI kneeling in prayer. The work, down to the lace ruffles, is wonderfully detailed.

(24) **Léon of Lusignan** (d.1393). The last king of Little Armenia before it fell to the Turks in 1375, his gisant has an enigmatically fascinating expression. Instead of a sceptre, he is clutching a pair of gloves.

(29) and (30) **Jean of France** and **Blanche of France**, beloved children of St. Louis, who both died, probably from illness, in 1243. The enamel plaques on their tombs are examples of a technique developed in Limoges in the 1200s.

(32) **Childebert** (d. 558). This statue, executed in the twelfth century, is in bas relief rather than fully dimensional. He is holding the model of a church in one hand, a convention usually reserved for Church founders. The fact that he murdered his nephews to gain control of Provence and Burgundy does not seem to have been held against him.

(33) **Clovis I** (d. 511). Sculpted more boldly than his son Childebert, only his mouth hints at the cruelty and deceit characteristic of his early reign. Clovis coped with his rivals and most of his relatives by having them killed, but in 496 he was converted to Christianity. After that he only murdered heretics.

(34) **Frédégund** (d. 596). Slave-born concubine queen of Chilperic I, she also solved disagreements by permanent elimination. Besides persuading Chilperic to send his first wife Gadswinna to her reward prematurely, Frédégund later dispatched her sister's husband and her own stepchildren. Her unusual tomb of copper and inlaid stone is probably nicer than she deserves.

(37) Although technically on the right side of the altar, the tomb of **Dagobert** (d.639) can only be seen from the left, standing on the stairs. The intricate carving under the arch tells the story of John the Hermit who dreamed that the soul of Dagobert was being carried off in a boat by demons but was saved through the intercession of several saints, including St. Denis. Although maligned in the French nursery rhyme that describes him doing silly things, Dagobert was a wise and just monarch. The corner statues of his wife Nanthilde and son Clovis II are nineteenth-century additions.

(44) **Henri II** (d.1559) and **Catherine de Medici** (d.1589). This multilevel tomb depicts their praying forms in bronze on top of the canopy and their discreetly nude figures at the moment of death on the grave itself. In the four corners are bronze virtues such as Justice. Henri, unfortunately, was

less charming than he looks, imposing a fanatical piety on everyone but his famous mistress, Diane de Poitiers. Jousting during some wedding festivities, he was speared through his helmet and a splinter reached his brain.

After his death Catherine took over, ruling through her four degenerate sons (also buried here): **François II**, **Charles IX**, **Henri III**, and **Alençon**. She ordered the death of Coligny, a prominent Huguenot, and thousands of other Protestants. Onlookers could not agree if during her reign she was masterful and realistic or panicked and confused.

(57) The last oversized tomb, of **Louis XII** (d. 1515) and **Anne of Brittany** (d.1514). As usual, the King and Queen are portrayed in prayer on the top of the temple-styled monument, which includes elaborate allegorical statuary around its base. The nude gisants, shown in their death throes, are unusually realistic and beautifully done.

One of the good kings, Louis XII was known as Father of the People. He eschewed extravagance and reduced taxes, claiming "I'd rather have them sneer at my parsimony than groan at my extravagance." Unfortunately he was a better poet than warrior and, going to war on Milan, lost all of Italy. After Anne died, he married a high-spirited princess of 16, but a few months of dances, late hours, and other activities sped him to his final rest.

After completing the upstairs tour, find the steps and go down into the crypt. This vault is an imposing edifice of stone arches, hanging lamps, and grillwork, behind which are bones and ashes recovered after the Revolution, including those of Marie Antoinette and Louis XVI. Shining black marble slabs, shockingly plain in contrast to the Rococo ornamentation upstairs, hold the Bourbon kings from 1600 on. The most famous of these was, no doubt, **Louis XIV**, The Sun King (1638–1715), but the best-loved was **Henri IV** (1553–1610), first of the Bourbon kings.

Henri IV, who converted to Catholicism with the famous line, "Paris is worth a mass," had all the characteristics which would endear him to Parisians. His nickname, Le Vert Galant, referred to his tireless pursuit of beautiful women, and he was a true gourmand who also wanted to see "a Sunday chicken in every pot." When he was stabbed to death by a religious fanatic, François Ravaillac, the incensed population systematically tortured the killer, then cut him up to feed wild dogs.

In the Square-du-Vert-Galant along the Seine, the willow that shadows Henri's statue is said to turn green before any other in the city. As with Louis XIV and Versailles, the greatest Bourbon kings have scattered their true monuments throughout Paris.

CHAPTER 16

SUBURBAN
Levallois,
Batignolles,
and Neuilly

▲ ▲ ▲

*And the world of the dead, like
a continent adrift, will move
farther and farther away from
the world of the living.*

—EDGAR MORAN
Man and Death in History

ALTHOUGH MOST PARISIAN cemeteries are on the
fringes of the city, a few seem farther out than others. The
arrondissements in which Levallois, Batignolles, and Neuilly are located are more residential, though only slightly
more distant from Paris than those of the other cemeteries.
While they may lack a certain historical cachet, they give a
good picture of the suburban cemetery: though their older
monuments are picturesque, the newer slabs of identical
granite appear as boring as the development homes which
can be found even in Paris.

To reach Levallois Cemetery, you can take the Métro to
Pont de Levallois stop and walk down Rue Baudin through
the town.

There are two graves of note in this patriotic burial
ground. The first is of a controversial patriot.

Opposite: Tomb of Raymond Millardet

LOUISE MICHEL *b. 1830, Paris; d. January 9, 1905, Marseilles.* Louise Michel is proof of the saying that cream always rises to the top, though in her case some people may feel that it curdled on the way. Louise, the daughter of a farmyard maid, was born at the country chateau of a wealthy French family. Her intelligence caused the family to take an interest in her. The son of the house taught her to read and write poetry, and she learned a great deal about gardening on her own.

As soon as she could, Louise set off for Paris, arriving at the city home of her benefactors. Attesting to her ability and education, they secured a teaching job for her in a girls' school at Montmartre, a position she held until she was 40. She continued to write verse which eventually caught the attention of Victor Hugo, who praised her highly.

Louise, who never did anything by halves, had strong socialist feelings which culminated in her participation in the 1871 Commune uprising. She fought on the side of the Communards, and when the regular army marched in from Versailles to quell the rioting she handed out cans of gasoline to set fires to sections of Paris—earning her the nickname of "Louise La Pétroleuse." When her defeated comrades began to flee, Louise called them cowards and fired cannon shot after cannon shot at the oncoming soldiers.

For her part in the insurrection she was given the death penalty, but, despite her urgings "to be treated like a man," it was commuted. She was exiled to New Caledonia, an island east of Australia. There she continued her good works, ministering to the needy and teaching the illiterate, until an amnesty was granted in 1880, and she returned to Paris. But she never returned to gardening or to teaching little girls; she was imprisoned several times for her part in Communist rallies.

Finally she moved to London. There she could be regularly seen in Hyde Park haranguing the conservatives. It was in London that she also wrote her *Memoirs* and a novel with the unlikely title *The Microbes of Society*. Her bronze bust surmounts three books, the third perhaps representing her poetry.

Known popularly as The Red Sister of Charity because of her kindness to the poor with whom she shared her small income, Louise was considered a mixed blessing. But she never wavered in her own beliefs. Pushing herself to the end, she died of pneumonia on a lecture tour in Marseilles.

Louise Michel is buried in the cemetery's circular center, on the left side as you approach it from the main entrance. After seeing her monument, retrace your steps to find the grave of composer Maurice Ravel. It is off the main road to the right of the entrance, four rows down and six rows in.

MAURICE RAVEL b. *March 7, 1875, Ciboure; d. December 28, 1937, Paris.* During much of his life, Maurice Ravel lived in the shadow of Claude Debussy. Music lovers assumed that Ravel was a mere follower of the older man, even copying his style. It is now clear that the influence was mutual, much as was Haydn's and Mozart's. Their personal relationship did not, however, share the geniality of their famous predecessors. While mutual respect never flagged, a strain persisted, fed perhaps by the pride each took in his own work and by their bands of excessively ardent supporters.

In appearance Ravel was likened to a jockey or a squirrel. Both descriptions seem apt, because he was small and alert and dressed like a dandy. He was also shy, and showed a love and affinity for animals throughout his life. Always self-effacing but never self-deprecating, he would frequently turn aside compliments by uttering humorous bird or animal noises.

In his youth Ravel supplemented his dandyism with an air of condescension and sarcasm, possibly as compensation for his small stature. For their renegade ideas and dress, he and his friends were known as The Apaches. In later life he dropped much of his aloofness, but he still remained shy and secretive. If he had love affairs of any kind, they have never become known. To his friends he displayed his keen wit and sense of loyalty, but he rarely allowed any outward display of strong affection.

The Ravel family was extraordinarily close-knit. From his mother Maurice inherited his love of Basque culture, especially its music. From his father, a gifted engineer who invented an early prototype of the internal combustion engine, he developed the intricate precision that characterized his music. Indeed, an admiring Stravinsky called him a "Swiss watchmaker."

The orchestral colorings of *La Valse* and *Daphnis and Chloe*, the vivid sense of place and action in *Alborada del Gracioso*, and the expert exploitation of style and line in the *Trio in A* all attest to his originality, strength, and innovation. Although Colette's text for the short opera, *L'enfant et les Sortilèges*, in which a naughty child is redeemed by tending to a wounded squirrel and eventually reunited with his mother, was not written for Ravel, it is easy to see why he wrote so movingly for it.

Ravel developed ataxia and aphasia, probably from a car accident in 1932. The symptoms (lack of coordination and memory loss) came and went, but their severity gradually increased. Finally he was unable to put on paper the music he had in his head. His mind generally remained clear, and he stood his condition stoically. Four years later, when a friend found him alone on a balcony and asked him what he was doing, he replied, "I'm waiting."

After another year his condition worsened considerably, and in December 1937 an operation was attempted. Eight days later his wait was over. Among his last words were, "I still had so much music to write."

To reach the second cemetery, Batignolles, take the Métro to Porte de Clichy and walk around the large high school to the cemetery entrance on Avenue du Cimetière. The easiest way to explore this cemetery is to head to the right on Avenue Circulaire and begin in Division 1. As with the other cemeteries, we will refer only to the divisions that are especially noteworthy, but we will not be going in strict numerical order because of the eccentric numbering at Batignolles.

DIVISION 1

The tomb of note here is that of **Jane Margyl**, the opera singer who died in 1907. The large sculpting shows her seated, eyes closed, reclining against the standing figure of a muse who holds a lyre in one hand and hides her grief with the other.

DIVISION 6

Lying only a few inches above ground is a mosaic portrait of extraordinary color which covers the grave of the painter **J. Péladan** (1858–1918). With his wild, curly locks and beard, the artist looks every bit the bohemian. Although Péladan was French, the mosaic lends a strong Russian flavor to his portrait.

DIVISION 2

Along the Avenue Centrale is the tomb of opera singer **Lucienne Breval**. In bas-relief on the headstone is a singer in the costume of an ancient warrior, leaning in sorrow on a spear whose point rests at the base of a headstone, as if to provide two views of the tomb at once.

DIVISION 25

Directly on the Avenue Centrale is the large rose granite monument topped by a cross of the famous Russian bass, **Féodor (Félix) Chaliapin** (1873–1938), a dark-browed giant of a man whose appetites for food, vodka, and women

were also gargantuan. Famous in the opera houses of the world, he also made over 450 recordings and even starred in a movie, *Don Quixote*, in 1933. Chaliapin had little patience with the Russian postwar government and moved his family to Paris a decade before he died there, yet his inscription reminds us that he was a *Fils génial de la terre Russe* (A gifted son of Russia).

Also in this section you may be startled to catch a glimpse of Harry Truman. The metal bas-relief of a bespectacled man wearing a bow tie is actually a French citizen known only as **Kuertz**.

DIVISION 26

In the upper part of this section, just a little bit in from the Avenue Centrale, is the grave of **Raymond Millardet** (1899–1931), which provides a wonderful wrought-iron sculpting with a three-dimensional silver biplane making a heavenly ascent under black iron clouds toward a glorious crucifix. Also in this section is the grave of another unknown personality, **Caurat**. The simple granite tomb is surmounted by a smooth, well-sculpted bust of a distinguished-looking man who nevertheless bears a distinct resemblance to the beloved comic strip character, The Little King.

DIVISION 31

Dead center in this division is the grave of the founder of surrealism, **André Breton** (1896–1966). Breton, an early French proponent of Freud, became a dadaist only to then combine those movements' philosophies with symbolism to form the basis for surrealism. He later published a famous manifesto, "Hands of Love." His grave is simple, topped only with a three-dimensional star and listing his name, dates, and the words *Je cherche l'or du temps* (I search for the golden times).

DIVISION 20

Walking back out of the cemetery on the left, you will find under the highway overpass the tomb of one of France's greatest poets.

PAUL-MARIE VERLAINE *b. March 30, 1844, Metz; d. January 8, 1896, Paris.* Beauty and the Beast. Remarkably ugly in feature and habit, Paul Verlaine produced poetry of extraordinary beauty. At their best they were a striking combination of form, nuance, and mood; poems which inspired and lent themselves well to settings by Debussy and Fauré. These are poems of mood and impression, of love and

BATIGNOLLES

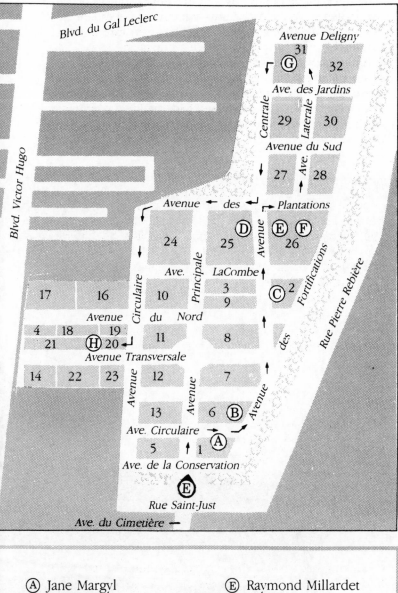

Ⓐ Jane Margyl
Ⓑ J. Péladan
Ⓒ Lucienne Breval
Ⓓ Félix Chaliapin

Ⓔ Raymond Millardet
Ⓕ Caurat
Ⓖ André Breton
Ⓗ Paul Verlaine

213

religious feeling. But they were born out of a life of drinking, violence, and promiscuity—a life whose decadent excess and unceasing self-destruction has rarely been matched.

Although Verlaine's father, Nicholas, was an army captain of exemplary behavior, his paternal forebears showed a predilection for the unsavory behavior Paul was to exhibit. His mother, Elisa, was consumed with the idea of having a child; indeed, her previous miscarriages were stored in

alcohol in the cupboard. Perhaps Paul's physical ugliness furthered her overindulgent maternalism; but, given her chance at motherhood, she doted on her son, spoiling him at every turn. The relationship produced a great ambivalence in Verlaine, ranging from expressions of deepest love to enraged, drunken attacks.

As a youngster he showed no special talent until he came across Baudelaire's *Les Fleurs du Mal* when he was 14. The book transformed his interests and his life. He became

Angel and cloud. Neuilly

obsessed with poetry. Eight years later, shortly after his father's death, he was published and became a member of a group of fellow poets known as The Parnassians. He was also beginning to show signs of alcoholism and sexual interest in men as well as women.

At 25 he began wooing Mathilde Maute, 16, with visits and love poems. Increasingly she fell under his spell, and they were married in 1870. But marriage could quell his desire for drink for only a few months. He soon took it up with increasing frequency and then with violence. He assaulted Mathilde when she was pregnant and once threw his infant son, George, against a wall.

By then he was already under the spell of Arthur Rimbaud, the 17-year-old poet who searched out Verlaine in admiration for his poetry but who soon took the upper hand in the relationship. Rimbaud's genius, looks, foul mouth, and penchant for the extreme seduced Verlaine from his family. The two drank, whored, and made love to each other while wandering through Europe. Rimbaud followed a philosophy of excess. So great was his hold over his friend that Rimbaud once made Verlaine hold out his hands so he could stab them. Rimbaud tried to pull out of the relationship, but Verlaine, increasingly agonized and unstable, threatened suicide. One night in Brussels, in a drunken rage, he shot Rimbaud. The wound was minor and although Rimbaud withdrew charges, Verlaine was sentenced to two years at hard labor.

It was during his time in jail that he experienced his religious conversion. Upon leaving jail he found Mathilde had separated from him. He made only a few half-hearted, unsuccessful attempts to see his son again. His conversion reformed him for a couple of years, but he soon fell into drunken obscurity. His poetry continued, erratic in quality but always human, even in failure.

In his twilight years Verlaine lived in squalid quarters relieved only by periodic stays at public hospitals. His body was giving way to his abuses: he suffered the effects of alcholism, syphilis, and gonorrhea. Hospital staffs treated him with deference, for his fame was growing. He was also kindly and pitiable, if unregenerate. Once the staff bought him a new overcoat for a public outing. Proud of his appearance, he had himself photographed wearing the coat. The next day he sold it to buy liquor.

Within his profession Verlaine became deified. But it was a strange and sorrowful apotheosis. Like some great and rare bird made captive by its own excesses, he was visited, exhibited, and admired. The honors for his success seemed really to be adulation for his past talent and pity for his present state. Admirers came and observed; their descriptions are plentiful, but all share an ultimate air of pathos. Verlaine, arriving late and loudly drunk for a dinner party, caused the already-seated Apollinaire to weep at his unknowing humiliation and at the waste of his genius.

The third cemetery, Neuilly, has an air all its own. The main walk, Allée des Ifs (Avenue of Yews), is bordered by high hedges and divides much of the cemetery lengthwise. The graves are located on numerous paths running off the main walk. Narrow portals cut out in the thick hedge of yews provide tantalizing glimpses of the tombs beyond, and walking through these dark entries makes for dramatic entrances. On the walls surrounding the cemetery are signs numerically ordering the rows.

The nearest Métro stops to Neuilly are Pont de Neuilly or Les Sablons. The main cemetery entrance is on the Rue Victor Noir; a side entrance is on the Rue des Graviers. A detailed map of the cemetery can be had at the conservator's office. Although they do not speak English, the conservator and his family are enthusiastically helpful.

DIVISION 1

Upon entering the main gate, one's attention is quickly drawn to a large statue of a woman peering forward while she holds the dead body of a half-naked man. Clearly the dominant figure of the two, she is also grasping a sword with her right hand.

Near the wall one is facing are the tombs of **Anzani** and La Monica. The Anzani headstone bears a decorative tree, the bottom limb of which is lying broken on the ground while the rest of the tree is flourishing in full leaf. Nearby trees and ivy enhance the effect of this design. **Francis La Monica**

(1882–1937) was a painter and sculptor whose tomb bears a sculpting, presumably by the artist, showing a barefoot woman kneeling on one knee, face and hands lifted to the sky. Viewed from the right-hand side we see a middle-aged woman in a shawl and kerchief, making a dramatic gesture. From the left her age and dress assume little importance, but the drama of the pose is greatly increased. It is a unique and affecting memorial.

Perhaps a little too formal to be classified as art deco, the tomb of **Abel Couvreux** (d.1922), otherwise unknown, provides an interesting example of early twenties style and decoration.

On row 320 near the back wall, which borders the Rue Jacques Dulud, we find a simple grey tomb with red lettering, marking the remains of a neighborhood resident, writer:

ANATOLE FRANCE *b. April 16, 1844, Paris; d. October 12, 1924, Paris.* Besides being known for *Penguin Island* and *The Red Lily*, Anatole France has gone down in history because of the size of his brain. During the nineteenth century proponents of the "more is better" school pointed proudly to the huge hat size of Georges Cuvier as proof that the bigger the cranium, the brighter the intellect. Posthumous measuring of celebrities' brains became an obsession.

Men of genius appeared to outweigh domestic servants until the deaths of Walt Whitman and Anatole France. Whitman's brain size equaled that of an average scullery maid; France's brain, even smaller, weighed in at 1.017, half the amount of Ivan Turgenev's 2.012. Unwilling to admit that the Russian was twice the writer, European scientists scurried back to the lab for some further refinements. Eventually the theory was refined out of existence.

Photographs of Anatole France show him as indeed small-headed, with a large nose, patriarchal beard, and wondering eyes. Although not a handsome boy, he had a happy childhood growing up on the quays of Paris, where his father was an established bookseller. France père was disappointed when his son did not continue the business, but Anatole had decided to write books instead.

He began his career with poetry and joined the most famous group of writers in Paris, The Parnassians. There he was tolerated until he produced a biography of favorite son poet Alfred de Vigny. Then he was welcomed warmly. Anatole continued with literary criticism and short plays, and around 1880 he published *The Crime of Sylvester Bonnard*.

By then he had married a beautiful young blonde, Valerie

NEUILLY

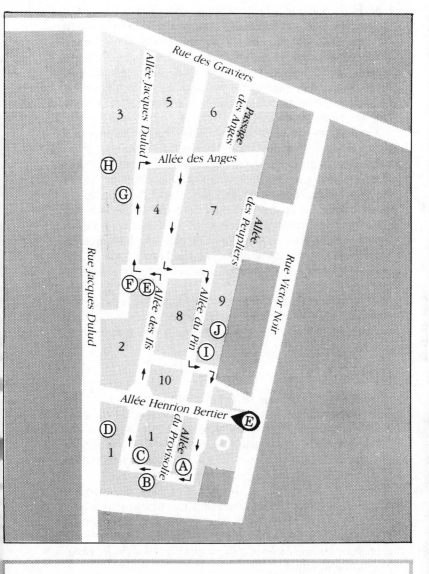

- Ⓐ Francis LaMonica
- Ⓑ Anzani
- Ⓒ Abel Couvreux
- Ⓓ Anatole France
- Ⓔ roses on a tomb
- Ⓕ Abbé de Cornille
- Ⓖ Reinach
- Ⓗ André Maurois
- Ⓘ Matillon family
- Ⓙ statue of woman

Guérin de Sauville. The following year his only child, Suzanne, was born. The Frances bought a charming home in Neuilly, and Anatole was professionally respected, financially secure, and happily married. The only thing he lacked—success in Parisian society—should not have mattered. But France pursued it with vigor, insistently adding himself to Mme Arman de Caillavet's salon. After making her his mistress, he divorced Valerie.

Unlike some artists who peak early, France continued to develop professionally until he died. The author of 35 books, he spent his last years surrounded by art treasures which he bought with the royalties that poured in. Two of his best books, *The Gods Are Thirsty* and *Penguin Island* were written when he was over 60 and had become increasingly less reluctant to take public stands on political issues. These stands were personal rather than literary. With the encouragement of Jean Jaurès, France sallied forth into politics as a socialist and came down hard in favor of Dreyfus.

In 1921, three years before he died, Anatole France was awarded the Nobel Prize in Literature. The nominating committee did not know that his brain was too small to deserve it.

DIVISION 2

Near the Passage des Ifs are two tombs of interest. The first is a small mausoleum with black wrought-iron grillwork on its door. Intertwined throughout the perimeter of the ironwork, at least during a springtime visit, you should find garlands of red roses. The combination of rich red on black metal is exceedingly beautiful.

Close to the corner is the grave of **Abbé de Cornille** (Curé de Ternes). His large sarcophagus bears on its lid the sculpting of a dead lamb. Through time a leg has broken off and lichen has begun to grow. At first startling and even grotesque, as one looks at it the sculpting has an increasingly emotional effect.

DIVISION 3

Along rows 100, 110, and 112 are small mausoleums belonging to various members of the **Saier** family, evidently prominent in the area. Each monument contains a stained-glass window with a different religious scene. Farther along, on row 40, is the tomb of another unknown, **Reinach**, notable for its large sculpting of a kneeling angel with stylised medieval curls who plays a lute with long artistic fingers, looking heavenward and singing.

Finally, four rows over on 36, is the plain black tomb of writer:

ANDRÉ MAUROIS b. *July 26, 1885, Elbeuf; d. October 8, 1967, Paris (Neuilly)*. André Maurois, born Emile Salomon Herzog, came to the vocation of literature late. He was 33 when his first collection of stories, *The Silence of Colonel Bramble*, was published. By the time he died at 82 he had over one hundred biographies and novels to his credit.

Throughout his life his best work was inspired by times of unhappiness. The happy days he spent in primary school, getting a master's degree in philosophy, and working in the family woolen mills yielded little literary material. It was not until his marriage developed problems that he began to write seriously. Maurois' young wife, Janine de Szymkiewicz, was startlingly beautiful but unstable. She felt smothered in the provincial mill town and suffered a breakdown.

André moved her back to Paris, but after World War II and the birth of three children, Janine's disturbance took a new turn. She abandoned herself to a manic round of nightclubs and spending. Maurois was trying to cope with this behavior when she died tragically of complications in her fourth pregnancy—throwing him into a deeper despondency.

To console him, Maurois' friends introduced him to a literary-minded young woman, Simone de Caillavet, the granddaughter of Anatole France's long-time mistress. Out of both marriages came Maurois' best novel, *Climats* (Atmosphere of Love), which details the hero's conflict between his love for his glamorous and temperamental first wife and his self-sacrificing second.

The years that followed were once again happy—but less productive—for André. The Maurois traveled, entertained, and spent a year at Princeton where he was delighted by the teaching life and his students. His novels and biographies of this period lack the emotional depth of his earlier writing.

World War II refueled him. He spent part of the time miserably exiled from Paris, traveling in the United States and in other parts of Europe. When he returned home, he was devastated at the way the city and his apartment had been plundered. The family factory had been gutted by fire, and his mother, arrested and then freed, had died shortly after her release.

In the emotional turmoil of rebuilding his life, André's writing again caught fire. His biographies of Victor Hugo, George Sand, and the Dumas family are considered excellent. His masterpiece, *Prometheus, The Life of Balzac*, was published when he was 80. He continued writing until he died two years later of an intestinal obstruction.

Maurois once speculated that the dead "live eternally in an artistic dream, endlessly creating a symphony of past and present memories." Standing at his grave one can almost hear the strains of his own melodious song.

DIVISION 9

The grave of the family of **Balve Lesport Matillon** is unique for its three sculptings of Mme Matillon. One is a full-length gisant showing even her sensible-heeled shoes. The other two are placed on the roof that covers her gisant: in the front a white marble bust, turbanned and looking reflective; in the rear, under a canopy with her dates (1833–1925), is a younger version with waved hair and pearls.

Behind Matillon and left, standing on an unmarked tomb, is yet another woman with eyes lifted skyward. The lines have a provincial simplicity, different from her more ornate sisters, yet the similarity of pose leaves one with the uneasy question: What are all these women looking at?

SOURCES

Abélard and Héloïse. D.W. Robertson, Jr. New York: Dial Press, 1972.

Adieux. Simone de Beauvoir. New York: Pantheon Books, 1984.

Alexandre Dumas, The King of Romance. F.W.J. Hemmings. New York: Scribners, 1979.

Anatole France. David Tylden-Wright. New York: Walker & Co., 1967.

Apollinaire, Poet Among the Painters. Francis Steegmuller. London: Rupert Hart, 1963.

Atlantic Brief Lives: A Biographical Companion to the Arts. Louis Kronenberger, Boston: Atlantic Monthly Press, 1971.

Au Père Lachaise. Michel Dansel. Paris: Fayard, 1973.

Auguste Comte. Arline R. Standley. Boston: Twayne Publishers, 1981.

Baudelaire the Damned. F.W.J. Hemmings. New York: Charles Scribners, 1982.

Beaumarchais. Frederic Grendel. New York: Thomas Crowell, 1973.

Bizet and His World. Mina Curtiss. New York: Alfred Knopf, 1958.

Camille Pissarro. Kathleen Adler. New York: St. Martin's Press, 1977.

Charmed Circle (Gertrude Stein). James R. Mellon. New York: Praeger, 1974.

Above: Napoléon's tomb

Chopin: His Life and Times. Ates Orga. Great Britain: Midas Books, 1976.

Cimetières et Sépultures de Paris. Marcel Le Clere. Paris: Hachette, 1978.

Colette, The Difficulties of Loving. Margaret Crosland. New York Bobbs-Merrill, 1973.

Corot. Keith Roberts. London: Spring Books, 1965.

David. Antoine Schnapper. New York: Alpine Fine Arts Collection, 1980.

Debussy: His Life and Mind. Edward Lockspieser. Cambridge: Cambridge University Press, 1978.

Debussy: Musician of France. Victor Seroff. Freeport: Books for Libraries Press, 1970.

Degas, His Life, Times and Work. Roy McMullen. Boston: Houghton Mifflin, 1984.

Delacroix. Yvonne Deslandres. New York: Viking, 1963.

Enfant Terrible (Maurice Utrillo). Peter De Polnay. New York: William Morrow, 1969.

France. Albert Guerard. Ann Arbor: University of Michigan Press, 1959.

Hector Berlioz. Victor Seroff. New York: Macmillan, 1967.

Jacques Offenbach. Alexander Faris. New York: Scribners, 1980.

Jean Paul Marat: A Study in Radicalism. Louis R. Gottschalk. Chicago: University of Chicago Press, 1967.

Jean Racine. Karl Vossler. New York: Frederick Unger, 1972.

Journey into Light (Louis Braille). Gary Webster. New York: Hawthorne Books, 1964.

La Fontaine and His Friends. Agnes Ethel Mackay. New York: George Braziller, 1972.

Madame Sarah (Sarah Bernhardt). Cornelia Otis Skinner. Boston: Houghton Mifflin, 1966.

Manet. Henri Perruchot. Cleveland: World Publishers, 1962.

Marie Antoinette. Desmond Seward. New York: St. Martin's Press, 1981.

Maupassant. Michael Lerner. New York: George Braziller, 1975.

Maurois, The Man and His Work. Georges Lemaitre. New York: Frederick Ungar, 1968.

Memoirs of Hector Berlioz. David Cairns, Ed. New York: Alfred Knopf, 1969.

Mistress to an Age. J. Christopher Hero. New York: Bobbs-Merrill, 1958.

Modigliani. Pierre Sichel. New York: Dutton, 1967.

Molière. Hallam Walker. Boston: Twayne Publishers, 1971.

Nadia Boulanger, A Life in Music. Leonie Rosenstiel. New York: W.W. Norton, 1982.

Napoléon Bonaparte. Vincent Cronin. New York: William Morrow, 1972.

Nijinsky. Richard Buckle. New York: Simon & Schuster, 1971.

No One Here Gets Out Alive (Jim Morrison). Jerry Hopkins and Danny Sugarman. New York: Warner Books, 1981.

Oscar Wilde. H. Montgomery Hyde. New York: Farrar, Straus & Giroux, 1975.

Pascal: The Life of Genius. Morris Bishop. New York: Greenwood Press, 1968

Piaf. Simone Berteaut. New York: Harper & Row, 1972.

Played Out, The Jean Seberg Story. David Richards. New York: Random House, 1981.

Poetry of Heinrich Heine. Frederick Ewen, Ed. New York: Citadel Press, 1969.

Prisoners of Honor: The Dreyfus Affair. David L. Lewis. New York: William Morrow, 1973.

Prometheus, The Life of Balzac. Andre Maurois. New York: Harper & Row, 1965.

Proust: The Early Years, Proust: The Later Years. George D. Painter. Boston: Little Brown, 1965.

Ravel, Man and Musician. Arbie Orenstein. New York: Columbia University Press, 1975.

René Descartes. Jack R. Vrooman. New York: Putnam, 1970.

Rousseau: The Self-Made Saint. J. H. Huizinga. New York: Grossman, 1976.

Seurat. Pierre Courthion. New York: Abrams, 1984.

Soutine. Raymond Cogniat. New York: Crown, 1973.

Stendhal. Joanna Richardson. New York: Coward, McCann and Georghegan, 1974.

The Affair of Gabrielle Russier. Mavis Gallant. New York: Knopf, 1971.

The Crazy Years, Paris in the Twenties. William Wiser. New York: Atheneum, 1983.

The Emperor's Talisman (Duc de Morny). Rosalynd Pflaum. New York: Meredith Press, 1968.

The Great Cities: Paris. Rudolph Chelminski. Amsterdam:Time-Life Books, 1977.

The Life and Times of Emile Zola. F.W.J. Hemmings. New York: Scribners, 1977.

The Lives of the Great Composers. Harold C. Schonberg. New York: WW Norton, 1970.

The New Columbia Encyclopedia. William H. Harris and Judith S. Levy, Eds. New York: Columbia University Press, 1975.

The New Grove Dictionary of Music and Musicians. Stanley Sadik, Ed. Washington D.C.: Grove's Dictionaries of Music, 1980.

The Real Isadora. Victor Seroff. New York: Dial, 1971.

The Space of Death. Michel Ragon. Charlottesville: University Press of Virginia, 1981.

Victor Hugo and His World. André Maurois. New York: Viking, 1966.

Voltaire. Jean Orieux. New York: Doubleday, 1979.

Women of Achievement. Susan Raven and Alison Weil. New York: Harmony Books, 1981.

INDEX

Permanent Parisians